JOURNEY
INTO
ONENESS

Other Books by Michael J. Roads

Talking With Nature
Journey Into Nature
Simple Is Powerful
The Natural Magic of Mulch

JOURNEY INTO ONENESS

Michael J. Roads

H J Kramer Inc
Tiburon, California

H J Kramer Inc
P.O. Box 1082
Tiburon, CA 94920

Editor: Nancy Grimley Carleton
Cover Art: Robert Wicki, courtesy of Ansata Verlag
Cover Design: Jim Marin-Pixel Media
Composition: Classic Typography
Book Production: Schuettge and Carleton
Manufactured in the United States of America
10 9 8 7 6 5 4 3 2

Library of Congress Cataloging-in-Publication Data
Roads, Michael J.
    Journey into oneness / Michael J. Roads.
        p. cm.
    ISBN 0-915811-54-5 : $10.95
    1. Roads, Michael J. 2. Religious biography—Australia.
3. Nature—Religious aspects. 4. Astral projection. I. Title.
BL73.R62A3   1994
291.2'12—dc20   93-38394
                                                                CIP

To my beloved Treenie.
The time of the Fairy Ring has arrived.

To Our Readers

The books we publish
are our contribution to an
emerging world based on cooperation
rather than on competition, on affirmation
of the human spirit rather than on self-doubt,
and on the certainty that all humanity is
connected. Our goal is to touch as many
lives as possible with a message
of hope for a better world.

Hal and Linda Kramer, Publishers

Contents

Acknowledgments

As always, my first thanks are to my wife, Treenie. She shares my universe, enriching my life. It is the nurturing energy of her love that inspires and ignites my writing.

To Hal and Linda Kramer, an especially big thank-you. Their faith in my metaphysical books is a part of their offering to the healing of the world.

When I learned that Nancy Grimley Carleton was to be my editor, I thought, "Oh dear, not another new one." Knowing that this would be a very difficult book to edit, I awaited the results. When they came I was surprised and very pleased. Thank you, Nancy; you were both sensitive and brilliant.

I also feel immense gratitude to the Spirit of Nature. The only way I can express this is by honoring our planet Earth on a physical level, and by encouraging a greater participation in the mysterious, mystical, intangible Nature that continues to elude our physical senses.

Introduction

A number of years ago I began what is probably the eternal quest — the search for Self. My path was very much one of Nature, as though preordained. At a certain point in my stumbling journey, I began to chronicle the remarkable events that were unfolding. This eventually found its way into a book and was published under the title *Talking With Nature*. Naively, I thought that this was the end of the matter, for my Self-searching seemed doomed by my inability to come to terms with my rapidly expanding reality. I was caught in the paradox of wanting to enlarge my reality but feeling frightened and confronted when it happened. Despite this, I continued to spend some time each day down by our nearby river, sitting on an old bridge board suspended out over the water for diving. Here mystical Nature most inspired me, so despite the challenges and the fears, I persisted!

Probably because of this persistence, there came a time when the Spirit of Nature entered my life, precipitating me from dallying by the river into a series of mystical adventures, each one more threatening, yet at the same time more revealing, than its predecessor. I documented these experiences in the book *Journey Into Nature*.

That was several years ago. During the intervening years, I have tried in vain to find a way to convey what has happened since. I have had to face the fact that it is impossible to simply tell my story exactly as it happened. Even before I consciously began my search for Self, life continually offered me the opportunity to expand my awareness by presenting me with metaphysical Doors. For me, these Doors appear where my accepted reality becomes hazy and undefined, presenting a subtle opportunity to enter a different, nonphysical realm. I have learned that there are rules of entry to be obeyed, the first of which is that you cannot take your physical body. Mystics have known and written about these mystical Doors throughout recorded history, but always they have shrouded and veiled them in mystery. Even the oft-quoted Doors or Gates to Paradise allude to the mystery of something wondrous that lies tantalizingly beyond our everyday normality.

I was aware of these Doors even as a small boy, when entering them was easy. In my innocence, I dreamed my way through them, experiencing glimpses of other realities without any need to understand. Some of those dream times took place when I was deeply asleep, but often I was wide awake, allowing myself to drift into some other, more magical space, losing all my awareness of the physical events surrounding me. When this happened during school classes, which was often, I could not remember anything that the teacher had been talking about.

As I grew older, developing my intellect and all the personal interests that clamored for attention, it became more and more of a challenge to find the Doors, let alone enter. For a while, lost in the process of being a young husband, father of four children, and a farmer facing the normal pressures of life, the Doors slipped away from my conscious awareness.

My decision in my early thirties to search for Self reawakened my relationship with the Doors. I became aware of the Doors once more when I went through the experiences I documented in *Talking With Nature,* but they remained distant, shrouded by the stress of everyday reality. Gradually, I learned of other factors involved if I was to approach the Doors as an adult. Of these, trust and timing were priorities, and trust determined the timing—trust in Self!

It took me a long time to find that trust. I discovered that just as I was a very practical, down-to-earth person, so also I had a far stronger, much deeper metaphysical aspect to my nature. I had to learn to trust this aspect. With the Spirit of Nature as my teacher, I gradually opened to the intangible, the invisible, moving closer and closer to the elusive mystical Doors. This time I was compelled to accept and embrace my expanding reality, not hide behind the discursive protection of daydreams.

During my journey into Nature, I discovered that when my consciousness left my physical body I retained a similar body composed entirely of Light. (We all have this light body.) In this body, I explored other dimensions of Nature. I became a participant in the mystical world of Nature, no longer living only in the physical world as an onlooker.

Introduction

As my search for Self took me ever closer to our human truth, so the Doors became clearer and more attainable, yet never for one moment was I able to pass through them into the Beyond. I learned that I had been approaching these particular Doors for lifetimes, but time and again I had turned away, distracted by the more obvious physical pleasures in life.

Eventually, after a process that often traumatized me, tested me, and left me emotionally wrung out, and which also gave me the greatest joy imaginable—a process that lasted many years—I experienced the realization of Self, of who I am.

And then the Doors, so long closed, opened.

❋

When I stepped through those Doors, linear time and corporeal reality ended. Everything of the known was abruptly replaced by an absolute unknown. Time, if it had any meaning at all, was spherical, so that all points of a sphere were the same time—always! Truly, an eternal now. Also, my reality was totally incorporeal, the rules of a normal reality utterly annihilated. Everything I experienced in that reality happened instantly. To borrow a linear term, let's say that a few hundred million years of life were graphically revealed, experienced, and rolled up into a single, spherical moment.

You see the dilemma of trying to tell it as it happened. As soon as I write the words of events in spherical time, I create linear time—and it was *not* a linear experience.

Introduction

After a few years, I decided that the book I wanted to write would never come to be. Then, one night, I leapt out of bed from a deep sleep, filled with insight and clarity. I was inspired to create an allegorical frame in which to present the picture of my story. For me, the essence of this story is wholeness, for life *is* holistic.

I have designed the allegorical frame to take an experience from beyond the confinements of time and present it in such a way that it is accessible, inspiring, understandable, and, I hope, enjoyable. However, let me clearly affirm that the characters in this book really do exist, or at least they do in my expanded reality! You can also be assured that the picture I offer is very definitely my own experience and truth.

Although this book is obviously a sequel to *Talking With Nature* and *Journey Into Nature*, it also stands clearly in its own right.

Michael J. Roads
Queensland, Australia

1
Thread of Connection

When I close my eyes,
exchanging seeing out for seeing in,
I see not only that which is possible
but also that which possibly IS.

The Doors, so long closed, opened.

I almost ran through those metaphysical Doors, only to skid to a stop in stunned surprise. As I passed through the portal, to my horror I raced out into an illumined nothingness. As far I could see in any direction—nothing! I glanced downward—nothing!

"Aaaaaaaah," I screamed in shock, waiting for the endless fall to begin, but nothing happened. I remained standing, tense but safe in this new and startling reality.

Reassured, I took a tentative step, my foot coming down firmly on illumined nothingness. This is ridiculous, I thought. Surely I'm supposed to become illumined, not walk around on illumination, or be swallowed in it. I needed time to ponder this mystery, but I was ironically aware that time no longer existed. I stood perplexed, unsure of what to do or where to go.

"I'm not sure I like this," I said aloud. I thought of my wife, Treenie. "I bet if she were here, she would manage something better than this," I muttered. Still a bit frightened, I resorted to the most basic instinct of all.

"HEEEELLLP!" I shouted as loud as I could, yet not a sound escaped my lips. I groaned, and in that moment I saw a stranger walking toward me, each step carrying the Being across not only the stars, but across whole galaxies.

I blinked a couple of times and stared in awe. I had been so preoccupied with my problem, I had not realized that I had been standing in space—or had I? Surely there had been nothing but illumination; now I was standing in a star-filled space.

No time passed while I watched a lean, human-height body that seemed to ripple and shimmer, yet gradually solidified as it came nearer. Suddenly, before me stood a Being unlike anything I had ever seen. It/he/she was upright and humanoid in form, yet appeared more like a huge regal cat than a human. Its eyes were large, glowing with a mellow silver light, as though some unearthly moon shone from empty sockets.

Recognition stirred. "You—you have the appearance of a sphinx," I said, feeling comfort and companionship from this creature of the stars.

It smiled a wide, easy smile in a face that seemed designed for smiling. The smile revealed teeth that were no more than a number of vestigial rows of a pale blue, oddly disconcerting by human standards.

"My name is Seine [pronounced C-ine]. I have come to be your teacher in the realm of realities you have now entered. I welcome you."

It held out its human-appearing hands, palms up, and automatically I placed my hands on them, palm to palm. I gasped as I was hit by an instant surge of recognition.

"Seine!" I shouted, "My God, Seine! Oh God, I didn't know you," and I fell into his arms, overwhelmed.

For endless moments we hugged. This hugging was unlike physical hugging, for although our light-body selves simulated the action, it was also an inner merging of Self, of becoming One on a level that transcends all normal hugging. My head spun as memories whirled and popped into my awareness like spheres of knowing.

I stepped back from Seine and just stared at him. He had always been masculine in my association with him, yet not male in the human sense of sexuality. His energy was masculine in intent and focus, yet as a Being he was neutral.

Pulling my gaze from Seine, I found myself looking at my own body. Everything about me seemed normal—my hands, fingers, feet, my whole body—yet in this other, nonphysical, reality I was composed of light, rather than the flesh and bone of physicality. I felt overwhelmed. I could accept being here, but when had I known Seine? It was obvious from the intensity of my feelings that we had known each other for a long time.

"What happened, Seine?" I asked. "What have I been doing for so long? I remember you as a close and loved friend, but there is so much I have forgotten."

His luminous eyes glowed with compassion. "Let it go, Michael. What you need will come back quickly, while the rest will surface in proper timing. It is enough that I am here, for you have many realities to encompass."

"Did you say realities? As in more than one?" I asked.

"Oh yes, to be sure. Reality is numberless and limitless. The only limit to reality is self-imposed."

4

I realized that although Seine appeared to be speaking to me, I was hearing him directly in my mind. There was no sound of a voice coming to me, just a direct inner hearing.

"Is this the way you hear me, as words in your head?" I asked him.

"Of course. You receive the words I form, yet you cannot intrude on my thoughts, nor can I intrude on yours. The words have to be formed and projected, and then we can communicate. In this way, we do not violate the individual rights of another Being."

"How far can the projected words carry?"

"As far as your reality can encompass," Seine replied.

I gasped. "Even across space and distance?"

Seine laughed. "Even across dimensions," he reminded me gently.

I felt numb. "I have forgotten so much," I murmured, "so much of who I am." My mind raced with a series of questions, but even as I formed them, answers also came. I looked Seine in the eyes. "Am I doing this, or are you?"

"I am aware without intruding that you are going through a question-and-answer phase. Most Beings experience this when they break out of the transient, illusory world into a universe of unlimited reality."

"Where are you from? How did you know I was coming through the Doors? Who chose you to be my teacher? Who decides on what happens to me now?" I was overflowing with questions.

Seine smiled inscrutably. In some peculiar way, his short, dense, golden body fur reflected the light of the millions of stars still swirling past around us.

"I'm from eternity," Seine replied patiently. "You told me you were coming through the Doors. You chose me as your teacher, and the decisions are yours," he added.

I frowned in concentration. "But I have no recollection of any of these things. Will I be able to remember?"

"You certainly will. Forgetfulness is a human habit. In fact, if you remembered all of your realities as Beings, you could not exist within the limits you accept as human. Your lost memory of eternity enables you to pass through the classroom you refer to as life on Earth."

"Eternity! You say that with so much familiarity, yet I have trouble even trying to comprehend it. How can you come from eternity?"

"Like you and like all humanity, and all the creatures and plants on your Earth, I was not born and I will not die. Is that not eternity, the birthplace and destiny of all life?"

"Yes, I suppose it is, if you put it that way," I said thoughtfully. "But what did you mean when you said I told you I was coming through the Doors. I didn't know myself until the moment I stepped through."

Seine stared at me pensively for a moment before replying. As I gazed into the fascination of his eyes, a filament of light seemed to roll slowly across their surface, then was gone, not at all like a quick blink. Again, it was oddly disconcerting.

He smiled, aware of my inadvertently broadcast thoughts.

"In your moment of Self-realization, when you experienced the death of identity, your knowing of Self swept every dimension of the All That Is. That *knowing* is the key to the lock of the Doors. You broadcast to every Being that you now experience a greater truth. That, Michael, is one of the most powerful proclamations that any human Being can make. I simply responded to your call as it radiated throughout all eternity."

I stood silent, trying to absorb the implications of what Seine had told me. He spoke of connectedness on a vast, universal, and multidimensional scale.

"Forming words and projecting them is a way of communicating in this and most other realities. On your physical plane, you vocalize words to create a sound, but the concept is the same. In this far more expanded reality, you can as easily form and project concepts and ideas, and even knowingness. Try to catch the knowing I am encapsulating and projecting to you now about eternity."

There were no words, but I felt as though I were being inflated like a balloon as a fulfillment of knowing flowed into my consciousness. Oddly, I had the feeling that I had always known everything I was receiving. It was like tasting a new fruit, yet as I bit into its newness, the juice was old and familiar. Despite this, I staggered with the enormity of what I encompassed.

"I apologize if that was a bit much. I wanted to test your capacities, and while I suspected they were considerable, you surprised me. What incredible potential you humans have. It always surprises me. What is even more stunning is how unrealized it is. How a race of Beings can live in a world where you each create your own reality and yet fail to realize it is just extraordinary!"

"Am I creating my own reality now?" I asked.

7

"Of course. Reality never stops, and neither does our experience. The paradox is that our experience creates our reality, and our reality creates our experience! By becoming aware of this, you can begin to choose your own reality."

"So if I have a reality of being surrounded by space and of standing on nothing, and I'm still feeling uncomfortable about it, is that my creation of reality?"

Seine laughed. "Your reality is a result of the shock you felt as you passed through the Doors. You literally felt empty as you faced a total unknown. Accordingly, your reality was an illumined nothingness. When you saw me, your reality encompassed space and stars. Would you prefer a more substantial reality?"

"I would prefer a more familiar one, say a nice meadow and stream, or a forest. Standing in space is a bit awesome when you have been earthbound for as long as I have."

"Look! Do you see the trees?" Seine asked.

Astonished, I now saw that all around me was forest, but what a forest! Although the trees appeared much the same as the trees of an everyday reality, their energy was quite different. Far from physical, these trees somehow resonated a spectrum of energy that seemed to merge with the deepest sense of peace and balance within my Self. I felt that the connectedness of trees and Self was enriched and magnified simply because for so long I had believed in separation — and by believing in it, I created it as a reality, aided and abetted by the rest of humanity. I knew that at some stage of Self, I had experienced Oneness with these trees; yet only by creating the illusion of losing that Oneness and experiencing the loss could I truly *know* what Oneness is.

"This, Michael, is the paradox of truth," Seine said, having inner-heard my broadcast speculation. "If you were unable to experience dark, there would be no way of knowing light. To experience light, we have to find it; yet, in truth, we *are* light, and we cannot lose what we are. To overcome this paradox, we create the illusions in life that reflect most strongly the depth of our perceptible separation from light, and having experienced this—over and over—we eventually find the flaw in our self-deception."

I stared at him, my mind whirling. If my years of farming had taught me anything, it was that nothing is really as it appears to be. As a farmer, I had seen Nature as an event taking place outside of myself, quite separate from me, yet all my later experiences had revealed that Nature is *not* separate from humanity. Only by experiencing the separation so powerfully was I able to recognize and assimilate the deep inner connection.

The volume of experiences that had taken me beyond the Doors had exposed the flaw in fixed, rigid belief systems. I now experienced truth to be an ever-expanding mode of infinite realities. The belief that humanity and Nature are separate is the very opposite of truth.

Seine reached out and put a comforting hand on my shoulder. "The beliefs you humans hold are the boundaries and barriers to your experience of God. There is no opposite to God, only opposition. The human belief in separation *is* that opposition, yet once again the paradox arises: It is the opposition to truth that reveals truth, for truth cannot be restricted any more than dark can contain or restrain light."

"What an irony," I murmured. "We attempt to validate an untruth by using logic and reason, and we come to believe in it. This, in turn, creates our reality, and we then live the reality of untruth until we expose its flaws, finally coming across truth—a light in the dark! And this is the way people live! This is how I lived!"

An immense sadness swept over me. The Spirit of Nature had taught me to shift my awareness from the normal space/time frame into a universe of endless possibilities. Who would teach those people who were totally closed to such possibilities? How many people were open to explore a new paradigm of endless potential? I was able to experience an inner state where Nature speaks in a voice of silence directly into my consciousness, but how many people are open to this possibility? My inner sadness had become a pain, growing with my thoughts—a pain unlike anything I had experienced before. I felt an inner weeping, as though some part of me were bleeding for humanity.

"Come!" Seine's voice was sharp as he walked away from me into the forest. I was abruptly wrenched from my inner hurt. I watched enthralled as the illumination of his Being blended and merged with the symphony of movement within the trees. He walked ahead of me, rather like a brilliant dust mote in a whirling spectrum of trees and light. I followed, not knowing where we were going, nor caring. Gradually, I learned to ease my way through the forest, becoming part of the dance of movement that now contained us. Seine seemed to flow and float as he walked, for although his legs moved in the rhythm of walking, the forest floor he walked on was at least a foot above the earth

I trod. I tried jumping, to see if I could land on the higher, more silent level where he strode, but it proved impossible.

For some unknown reason, our pace was steadily increasing, and soon I was kept busy simply keeping up with him. Faster we went, and faster, hurrying through the forest like silent shadows, until, just at the moment I was going to protest about this mad rush, I suddenly saw Seine sail up and up into the air, as he leapt easily over the vast trunk of a fallen tree. I ran as hard as I could at the tree trunk, gathering myself for a leap that under normal physical conditions would have been completely impossible.

I jumped, soaring up and up, over the huge log—and down the other side. There was no forest floor.

❋

I fell, tumbling over and over, listening to the silent cry of my own voice—not a cry of fear, but of utter bewilderment. I tumbled through time and space, light and dark, up and down, and I kept falling . . . falling . . . falling.

Somehow, as I fell I was able to relax, surrendering to the experience, and as I released my falling slowed. I could see beneath me a huge illuminated pool of what I could only describe as energy, with the illumination coming from a single, powerful source of light. Into this swirling matrix of energy, I fell. When I landed, safely and easily, I was bewildered to find that the energy pool was the farm I had owned and worked on many years previously when Treenie and I had lived in Tasmania.

As I stared around me, even more disconcerted, I be-

11

came the dual experience of me in the past, a farmer, and Self of Now. As the farmer I saw only a farm with all its attendant problems. As Self, I experienced the matrix of illumined energy expressing itself through all the complex forms that make up a farm. As Self, I saw that the illumination had a program preset into a nonphysical energy control. This control had the capacity to allow farmer-me to alter the program at will. The energy control was also the source of illumination for this huge pool of latent, receptive energy.

As Self, I saw the problem farmer-me faced. Farmer-me had no knowing of an energy pool that manifested as cows, soil, pasture, and all the vast array of micro and macro life forms that compose a farm—Nature! As farmer-me, I saw and related to the farm and Nature in purely physical terms, yet Self knew that the physical farm was no more than a biological reflection in a mirror of consciousness. The preset program in the energy control could not be reached physically; it was metaphysical energy. Self knew that the programmed matrix of energy was the birthplace of infinite, unlimited potential, yet, by design, the physical farm could only yield its potential according to the setting in the energy control, the source of illumination. As farmer-me, I was faced with the task of changing that setting without knowing that such a possibility existed. Thus we stood in the center of the farm—a duality: my Self, an aware fusion of light-as-movement at the center of a vast pool of energy, and farmer-me, an unaware physical man trying in my daily farming to increase the farm's productive potential by using exploitive techniques.

12

To achieve the increase in production, farmer-me spread chemical fertilizers into the matrix of energy/physical farm. By introducing chemical manipulation, Self observed that farmer-me caused a reaction in the pool of energy. This produced a twofold result. First, there was an increase in production, accompanied by a ripple of discord in the environment. This, in turn, led to an increase in various cattle diseases and an even greater separation from Nature.

There was no quick and easy way out. Calling Seine for help was out of the question! The only solution was to begin a program to enlighten farmer-me and change his farming practice by changing his view of life. And so I began — or tried to begin. As Self, I talked to farmer-me, speaking truth into his heart. He was receptive, but as I whispered into his heart, my silent words were drowned by the crescendo of negative thoughts that roared like a whirlwind through his mind. Self experienced shock, having forgotten this aspect of the farmer-me past. As Self, I eased back from the pressure I had been applying to farmer-me. I realized that a patient, persistent, gentle approach was required. Besides, he was me! This was the ultimate irony. I, as Self, was now teaching the farmer-me of nearly two decades ago! To think that I had once believed in orderly illusions like time!

As Self, I reached out into the All, and I reeled in shock. I encountered the expanded Self of countless numbers of humans encouraging the identity self of that moment as they struggled toward Self-knowing. Surely, the paradox of all paradoxes. The higher Self that I, and others like me, had struggled to reach was never above or beyond, or in the distant future, but the truth of who we are, right here and now. A quantum leap was required, a *real* surrender in consciousness, not a conceptual surrender of the intellect.

I, Self, laughed and laughed. What matter time? I had all the time in the world for Michael, the farmer-me of the past. In fact, only by changing farmer-me of the past could I become the Self of Now! If only I had known—if only any of us knew—that the person we are now is a composite of many selves from beyond time, space, and separation. Out of the physical world, linear time is without meaning. People are locked into the belief that our past affects our future, while in reality our future has just as much effect on our past. And the key to all of this is the present!

I connected with farmer-me using Treenie and Nature. It was Treenie who first introduced the idea of gardening organically, an idea that I, as farmer-me, soaked up like a sponge. I often wondered how I, a person who languished at the bottom of class at school, should suddenly find that I had an ability to comprehend instantly a subject that was so new to me. To Self, it was old hat!

It was Treenie who first made a conscious connection with the dairy herd, an event that was to change completely the way I, as farmer-me, related to cattle. It was Treenie who encouraged me to make an agreement with the various forms of wildlife on the farm, withdrawing all violence in the forms of poison and guns that I had been using in pest control. Treenie was ever open and receptive to her intuition as her insight deepened and expanded.

As Self, I also used Nature in my efforts to reach farmer-me. As farmer-me, I had a festering hatred for carrion crows, shooting them on sight when I had my gun. I was revolted by the crows' habit of picking the eyes out of dead and dying cattle. One particular cow had been paralyzed when calving, and because she was in an inaccessible place, owing to the steep hills and valleys on the farm, I was forced to attend to her where she lay. Normally, as farmer-me, I would roll the cow onto a tractor carry-all and take her back to the farmstead for treatment. However, due to the circumstances, each day I slithered down the long steep slope to the bare half-acre of land this awkward but favorite cow had chosen to calve in. Twice a day I hand-milked her and rolled her over to a new position. Then I toiled back up the slope to complete my long day's work. For a week it seemed that the cow was well on the way to recovery, eating and drinking the food and water I carried to her. One morning, I saw before I reached her that she was dead. A crow flew sluggishly away from behind her head, and I hurled a stone at it in futile rage.

The cow lay stretched out on her side, still warm, the upper eye socket empty and bloody. As farmer-me, I sat and cried, sobbing from both frustration and a sense of loss. I felt cheated and empty. Into this emptiness, I, Self, focused my knowing, flooding farmer-me with an inner peace. As Self, I felt this knowing within my farmer-self, as my inner vision opened to insight.

As farmer-me, I stirred, impelled by an odd realization. I had a sudden inner knowing that crows only congregated around cows who would eventually die. I had noted that for the week of my ministering to this cow, crows had always been in the immediate vicinity. I thought back to similar situations in which other cows had died. Yes! Always a few crows hung around, no matter how long the wait.

I remembered the small Jersey cow who had fallen over the edge of a steep cow track. She had received serious cuts and deep scratches and had dislocated her shoulder. As farmer-me, I had given a mighty flat-footed kick to the bulging shoulder, and it had popped back in place with an audible crack. Any delay would have caused such massive swelling that it would have been impossible to relocate. I treated the injured cow on the spot twice a day for nearly two weeks before she eventually staggered to her feet, to emerge battered but alive. Sitting reminiscing, I remembered very clearly that I had never seen a crow in attendance. There were other cows at other times, but always the same realization held true.

Realizing this as farmer-me, my insight revealed that in Nature all is known. A crow knows which animal will live and which will die. This knowing was part of what it meant to be a carrion crow. With this insight, my judgment-based hatred died. A dung beetle buried animal dung—that is what it did. A carrion crow knew which sick or injured cow or sheep was to be carrion even before death, and the taking of an eye happened only moments before or after life finally fled the form. With insights such as this, an openness to Nature and life blossomed in farmer-me, but it was uphill work!

Early one morning on my way to milk the cows, when

I was in a quiet, pensive mood, as farmer-me, I stepped onto the merry-go-round I had made for my children. As I spun around, vulnerable and open, Self spoke a clear and profound question into my consciousness: Who am I? This question hit me with the power of a thunderbolt. With it came more questions, simple but profound. What am I doing on this planet? What is life? What is my place and purpose in all this? Am I born to simply work, procreate, and then die, wondering what it's all about? Who am I?

I jumped off the spinning merry-go-round and went in to Treenie. "This may sound stupid, but I just realized that I don't know who I am," I said, sharing my inner dialogue.

"That's incredible. I've been asking myself the same question," Treenie replied.

"Well, I want to know—right now," I said firmly.

As Self, I smiled. I was ever impatient. The process, however, was well underway. Into farmer-me's consciousness, the idea of wholeness formed into a bud, and over a number of years, it came to flower. These were not easy years, and they came with many painful lessons, but once the seed of wholeness took root, its progress was inexorable.

As farmer-me, I learned that the exploitation of Nature created a discord that only led to my own downfall, and so I learned to harmonize with the natural rhythm and flow of life on a farm. I learned that my farm had many levels of reality. One reality was the farm as physical; another was the farm as a latent pool of energy, with a metaphysical energy control. Through everyday experience and observation, I learned that physically, no matter how or what force was applied, the control that directed the pool of energy could not be touched. As farmer-me, I learned to listen to the whisper of my heart instead of the shout of my mind. I learned to trust my intuition, and Self, the inner teacher, was more easily able to reach me. I asked the question: Who preset the control? I heard the answer from deep within: We did. In what possible past did we set it? In a probable future. Where do the possible past and the probable future connect? In the vast swirling matrix of energy we call Nature. So how do we reach the control?

This was the question Self had been waiting for. Into the receptive consciousness of farmer-me, an incredible design of concept and vision gradually grew, filled with the promise of meaning. My awareness expanded: I am a farmer, yet I am One with All Life. This farm is not separate from me; thus it is as responsive to me as are my children. The preset control may be changed only by the power of love.

Then came the paradox. There is a timing to any alteration of the control. The fact that farmer-me had consciously realized its potential did not automatically mean that it was right timing to alter the setting. Very clearly, as farmer-me, I perceived that my insight and vision had spelled out the end of my farming career. Just as love could alter the setting of the control, so could the truth of love reveal the timing.

As farmer-me, I saw clearly that a new, holistic expression of agriculture was required before the latent potential reached its right timing. I had a lot of inner growing to do!

Together, Treenie and I made the decision to quit farming. Together, we would set out to find the answer to our question: Who am I? We knew that this was the key to the human timing of that patient, powerful potential.

With this realization bursting like a meteor shower into the vision and awareness of farmer-me, . . .

✳

. . . I, as Self, completed my jump over the huge log to land gently and easily on the forest floor. Seine smiled at me with a look of tolerant amusement.

"Wow, Seine! That was some jump! But why?"

"You asked a question with such a degree of sadness that you created the experience. You asked who would teach those people who are closed to their higher potential. As a farmer, you were such a person, yet you became your own teacher. People are never without help from Self or other Beings. The help is always there, but of course, if you are closed and unreceptive, then you create and maintain your own helplessness."

The light that flowed around Seine was a living green, almost seeming to caress him as it pulsed from the forest trees, making contact with him. I, too, was similarly surrounded by the heart-light of the living forest.

"Where was I when all this happened?" I asked, yet even as I asked, I knew. "It all happened in the brief no-time of making that jump, yet in linear time, years passed by. And I was not alone. The Nature of this metaphysical forest connected with the farm in the same way that I of Now connected with the farmer-me of then. Wow! We use the word Oneness as though it is a something, a concept, but the reality of Oneness—and the implications. It's incredible!"

Seine reclined on a branch of the fallen tree.

"What did you learn, Michael? What did the experience teach you?"

Sitting down on the forest floor, I leaned back against the trunk, my fingers digging into the dirt. Yes, it was real! I glanced up at Seine. As I watched him, the film of light slid slowly across his eyes once more. This had the odd effect of illuminating the silver light of his eyes. I took my time as I recollected the experiences.

"I was surprised by many aspects. It never occurred to me that we could be our own teachers. The fact that a future Self could help a past me would have seemed a farfetched fantasy. I remember that moment on the merry-go-round so clearly. The question 'Who am I?' seemed to come from within with startling power, yet I never dreamed that my future Self was the author of that question."

Seine smiled. "This fundamental question cannot be asked until the answer itself lies within the consciousness of the person who asks. What else?"

"Even more powerful than that was the experience of Oneness. I witnessed a thread of connection between farmer-me, the Self of Now, the farm and all its Nature, plus all the dimensions and aspects of being that were involved."

Seine's eyes seemed to sparkle. "And did you recognize that thread of connection for what it is?"

"Yes. The connection is consciousness."

"Excellent."

Seine reached out and touched my shoulder, and instantly we were standing in a beautiful park. Nearby, a waterfall flowed from a formation of rocks, disappearing as it flowed into a small rainbow. I was fascinated. The rainbow was formed by the play of water, yet in some mysterious way, where the rainbow touched onto the rocks, the water simply vanished. I stared, trying to comprehend.

"Balance, Michael. A natural manifestation of balance."

Seine's voice was silent, a projection of thought into my consciousness, yet for some reason it triggered a sudden explosion of memory.

"Altares!" I shouted. "That's where I last saw you. We were involved in the manifestation of a liquid that could flow independently of any planetary gravity." My eyes went round and wide in astonishment. "And we did it!" Suddenly, another memory surfaced, one I had tried to suppress some years ago. I remembered Seine from one or two of my early metaphysical experiences. I had not had the vaguest recognition of him then, and unable to rationalize my experiences, I had stuffed them into the already-crammed compartment of my psyche that contained my undealt-with issues.

I now felt a vast relief as more of the contents of that compartment were released.

"Seine, why have I been wasting my time on Earth? I don't belong. It is not my home. I have vague memories of other Beings and intelligent races light-years ahead of humanity."

"But not separate, Michael. Never separate. Always the thread of consciousness connects. Earth was your choice, just as long ago in linear time, I, too, lived many spans on that beautiful planet in a civilization well before the present one. And, I might add, I have had an occasional incarnation there during the present ages. But again, never separate. This is your lesson: to experience the vastness and completeness of the One, and yet—again the paradox—to realize Oneness is also movement and growth, for consciousness seeks always to expand. Truth cannot be static. You must experience and encompass this."

I felt an instant wariness as I recalled jumping over the log. "I hope I won't be lured into leaping into situations that reduce me to ... to ... "

"Awareness perhaps," Seine cut in, "or expansion. You call that a reduction? Can the experience of your greater potential really be a reduction?" He laughed at me, his strange silver eyes luminous with mystery. "I can only tell you the same truth you already know, a truth that applies to all humanity at all times: You choose your experiences in life, and not choosing is also a choice!"

"More paradoxes," I sighed. "It's all paradoxes, one after another."

"All to be lived," said Seine. "Come with me." He turned toward a large building that loomed very tall, needle slim and elegant, nearby.

2
The Last Elm

To bow before a humble tree
takes but a moment of our time,
while that which we may receive
fills all the spaces of eternity.

As Seine and I walked toward the building, once again threads of memory struggled to rise above the fog of Earth time.

"I've been here before," I said.

Seine nodded, without replying.

"This is a Temple of Learning, one I've been in many times." I reached out to touch the smooth, silvery exterior of the building, but my fingers met with no resistance. Then I remembered. I reached out again, but this time my fingers were an extension of my whole focus, rather than a merely curious touch, and the building was unyielding, glass smooth, and faintly warm. A strong impression of the building being alive flowed into my fingertips, yet it was not *a* life; rather, it was the molding of life, of thought and form meeting in this wondrous and beautiful needle of architecture, a cradle of creativity.

Seine had already entered the building, so I followed him, passing through the open doorway into fluted, flowing archways and light, open halls. A mystique pervaded the interior, a feeling that what I might expect and what would be revealed would be very different. Seine had gone ahead of me into some other part of the hall, but rather than search for him, I decided to look at the large mural on a distant wall. How such a wide interior could be contained in such a narrow exterior puzzled me, but as I approached, my attention was held by the energy and power of the mural.

As I reached the mural, I gasped. It was a picture of a huge tree, but the image was holographic. Although the size made the tree appear to stand alone, it actually stood in a small copse, surrounded by other trees of different species.

"It's an English elm," I murmured in surprise.

I stood back to regard this solitary elm, stunned by the size, impact, and sheer overwhelming reality of the mural. As I stared, a slight breeze seemed to ruffle its leaves, and the tangible humus smell of a thriving ecosystem became apparent. Intrigued, I walked to one side, wondering if I'd find an opening into some magical wood, but, no, the dimensional image faded, and the tree appeared flat. However, once I faced it again, it breathed with life and vitality. Almost as though following an invitation, I reached out tentatively to touch a limb of the great elm.

※

My arm became an outreaching branch, one of many branches spreading around me. I was a mammoth specimen of English elm, my branches reaching over fifty yards up and out toward the sky. I was Elm, yet my awareness of Self was undiminished. I stood alone in a small copse of trees, and I was aware of an aloneness that was almost alien to my human Self. I was the last English elm on planet Earth! I felt a surge of horror, yet Elm contained the knowing with equanimity. Elm felt no emotion, no fear of death or dying, no alienation, nothing other than a sense of profound aloneness. Through Elm, I discovered the difference between separation and aloneness. Alone I stood, more alone than any member of any species should ever have to be, yet the Elm's knowing of Oneness was as powerful as life itself. Not even the vaguest hint of separation flickered in the consciousness of Elm, just aloneness within Oneness.

My Elm consciousness reached out across planet Earth and beyond, connecting with the countless stars in unnumbered galaxies. Yet I was grounded, a conduit for energies and influences beyond knowledge or understanding. My Elm role was unique, for, as with all tree species, I expressed a different vibration of the One, the Godhead of All Trees. As Elm, life was a weaving, creative rhythm of consciousness, while each human was a mode of consciousness struggling to express its individuality through a physical framework, yet hampered by its separation from the One. Every species of tree, plant, and creature existed as a blend of consciousness, unborn and undying. Each tree form was a physical touchstone with the physical Earth, each species a form of splendid physical evolution as it followed the design its tree spirit expressed in each different species.

I became aware of Elm as more than a tree, for beyond

26

the form of Elm was an architect of form, a Being that somehow contained Elm within its own consciousness, yet at the same time was contained by Elm. I realized that Elm, like all trees, was a synthesis of Being. With human eyes, we see a physical tree, yet this physical tree is only the biological reflection of a spiritual energy that expresses itself through each species of tree. Just as it is I who express through my toes, my fingers, and each hair on my body a unique creation that is the physical me, so, using the body of Earth, other Beings express their uniqueness through the different location of trees. Through this Elm Being, I connected with the spirit and intelligence of all Elm. My awareness focused on the Being, yet there was no hint of form. All that I could perceive was a Being of Light and, within this ethereal "substance," the movement of energy. And beyond this, I was connected with the intelligence of this Being in a way that defies description. I was Self— and Elm.

As Elm, my Self-awareness reached out to a small group of humans who had come trudging into the clearing beneath my branches. Unknown to them, our consciousness mixed and merged, for I was the focus of their attention.

Like most people, they did not realize that their thoughts create a focus, and that no matter what the subject, they connect in consciousness with what they are thinking about. And they were thinking about the elm.

"So what are we gonna do about it, Gus?"

The person who posed this question was a young man named Billy, barely out of his teens, but the anger and violence that flared in bright red flashes around him was the result of a multitude of confrontations with injustice. For many lifetimes, he had fought against injustice, as fatally attracted to it as a moth to the flame. Of the half-dozen people, two others, Tom and Hans, felt the same attraction. Any issue that was termed unfair was their unwitting fodder.

Elm had no intellect, no mode of reasoning, no inkling of separation, no emotions, no sense of injustice—simply a connection with All That Is—a connection based not on knowledge, but on Beingness. Within Elm lay an untapped reservoir of vast wisdom, yet this wisdom had never been translated into human terms. Elm's knowing was the pure essence of spirit, undiluted and pristine. Elm felt the discord of the mixed group of people. Not discord as bad or good, for it was without judgment—just discord.

Gus was an older man in the group, wiser and more moderate. His consciousness reflected the pale yellow of deep anxiety, but his anger was finished, long ago burned away. He was accompanied by his two daughters, Faye and Jeanne, both with loving dispositions.

"What do you suggest, Billy?" Gus asked, his sweeping glance including Tom and Hans.

Billy, Tom, and Hans exchanged meaningful glances, and in their consciousness, I read their resolution. They meant to harm another human. Their intent radiated as a dull gray mist, roiling around them in folds of negativity.

"I reckon we ought to bash the bastard." Billy spoke quietly but vehemently, while Tom and Hans nodded.

"No!" rose a shout of protest from Faye. "Violence isn't the answer. Isn't violence the very thing that we most detest?"

The Last Elm

As Self/Elm, I marveled at human deceit. This group of people was almost devoid of any comprehension of their intent, yet it radiated forth, shouting its message to all of Nature. In consciousness, every tree in the copse, every bird and animal, every insect could, each in its own way, read the intent of this group of humans. Nor did there arise any animalistic reaction or condemnation from Nature to this intent; there was simply a knowing in consciousness. Humanity, however, lost in the smother of intellect, blinded by a multitude of personal fears and the isolation of each person's separate reality, knew nothing of this.

"Listen, Faye, and you, Jeanne. You don't have to be involved in this—you don't need to know any details—but I, for one, cannot stand passively by and let that bastard cut the tree down. For Christ's sake,"—Billy's voice rose to a loud and angry shout—"this is the last elm that anyone knows of." His voice barely under control, he continued. "Just because the tree is on Joel's land, that's not a license to cut it down. My God, the last elm! I . . . I'll shoot him first." He glared his defiance at the group.

"That's quite enough of that sort of talk, Billy," Gus warned. "Your anger is going to get you into trouble one of these days. Faye's right. Using violence defeats our purpose, and it generates even more violence. It just goes on and on. I'm sure we can get Joel to see reason if we approach him again."

"Oh yeah!" Billy snarled. "And what good has it done the last three times? Three times, I'm telling you! Ever since he was offered a fortune for the timber of the last elm, money is all he cares about. I'll shoot the bastard!"

Aggression, anger, helplessness, shame, sorrow, loss, frustration—all these emotions and more swirled in a miasma around the group of people and Elm. Elm knew none of these emotions, for all became discord as they impinged into the consciousness of Elm. In Elm, this discord was subtly transmuted, vibrating higher and finer into the aura of harmony that was the natural expression of Nature. I knew that with the destruction of each tree this natural transmutation of negative energies would become more and more restricted, until eventually humanity would be forced to confront its own most base and negative reality. I shivered at the prospect, leaves trembling along my branches and twigs.

Jeanne looked up, staring at the tree in concern. "The elm can hear us," she said softly, shyly. "It feels our concern. Maybe it knows it's the last elm left. What a terrible weight to bear."

"Don't be soft, girl," Billy said angrily. "Trees don't know anything. They're just dumb, inanimate things waiting to be cut down and used."

"Why do you care, Billy?" Faye asked perceptively. "You don't have any real feelings for the trees; that's obvious. Are you in this just for the fight? Someone to get angry with? Is that all it means to you?"

"That's enough." Gus intervened before Billy could reply. "Squabbling among ourselves isn't going to help. Let's be getting home. I suggest we all think very carefully about this and plan a moderate, sensible approach to stop Joel from cutting the tree down."

The group walked quickly away, yet their distance meant

nothing to Elm. For as long as their focus was on Elm, their consciousness continued to radiate their intent as clearly as if they sat in my branches.

Nights and days passed, unmeasured and unheeded. Time was meaningless; only the seasonal rhythms remotely resembled the passage of time to Elm. However, only a few days after the group had departed, a single, deeply troubled human approached. I knew that Joel heralded the demise of Elm—the last English elm—but Elm was not disturbed. Only the discord of the moment had any import, the discord that preceded action. Neither was physical action of any real importance; the only active representation of reality was the movement in consciousness.

Everything about Joel was broadcast in his troubled consciousness, and I read his story with the ease of reading a book. He had been offered the staggering sum of a million pounds for Elm by an unscrupulous businessman who planned to make a personal fortune from the last Elm. Despite what Billy believed, Joel was very much a man with a conscience, and right now he was deeply troubled. He badly needed the money, yet everything in him abhorred selling the tree. His wife had left him four years ago, going off with another man, and Joel had custody of their only daughter, Nadine. Nadine had developed a serious tumor of the brain, and only immediate surgery in America could give her even a slim chance to live. During the time it had taken for the surgeons to determine the best procedure and schedule an operation date, Joel had been contemplating cutting down the Elm. The thought appalled and repelled him, yet he was terrified that without the money and operation, Nadine would soon be dead. Very few people knew of the inner struggle Joel faced every day. Only the business deal had leaked out, and he was now the local Mr. Bad Guy. For himself, Joel did not care. He was a taciturn, withdrawn man, not good at communicating and easily misunderstood. All the love he had was focused on his beloved Nadine. To lose her would be the end of his own life. He could delay no longer. Only yesterday the surgeon had phoned to advise that surgery must take place within hours. For Joel, sweating on the decision was now over.

With trembling hands, he pulled a small can of deadly tree-kill poison from his pack, and digging down to some of the larger roots, he drilled a hole into them and poured in the poison. He cried softly all the while. His crazy logic tried to protect him by reasoning that if the tree were dead, it would not matter if it were cut down. This was self-deception to a high degree, but because the guilt and pain were more than he could endure, as crazy as the reasoning was, the plan might work. Soon, his mind could mercifully blot out the truth, burying it deep in the pool of his subconscious.

Elm felt the poison as a rapidly developing surge of discord—a discord so great that as it died, every tree on the planet felt the withdrawal in consciousness of the last Elm on Earth. Again, there were no feelings of retribution, no desire for revenge, no judgment, not even a fleeting feeling of regret. Elm was an expression of life. Life continued, even if the physical form could no longer continue to express it.

Although I was aware it took days for the leaves to wither and fall, the sap to thicken and stop flowing, in consciousness Elm withdrew very rapidly. For many years a killer disease had decimated the elms of Earth, and as the last one left, Elm was ready for the next step in the movement of Elm consciousness.

But for the people involved, the tragedy had only begun. Although Joel had been faced with an agonizing choice, Nadine died during the operation. When, a few days later, a single bullet murderously blew the back of Joel's head into a bloody pulp, this act only foreshadowed the suicide he had already planned. Billy, so obviously guilty by having broadcast his intent to all who would listen to him, was sent to prison for life, yet he was innocent. Nobody ever suspected the more subdued, controlled violence of Hans, nor did they have any clue about why Hans hanged himself three months later. All the repercussions of violence played themselves out, gradually draining the anger from the global pool of consciousness. And all so totally futile. Elm knew nothing of this. Although I followed the tragic repercussions, to Elm it was meaningless. Elm related to life in terms of consciousness; discord and harmony each carried countless nuances on endless dimensional levels as Elm merged with the vast oceanic consciousness of One.

With Elm, I released the physical form of a tree, merging into the omnipresent consciousness of All That Is. Although I no longer had an Earth form in which to express, yet this was no death. Elm was unborn and undying, merely waiting for a vibrational pull that would clarify the next physical or nonphysical expression of its consciousness.

With Elm, I became aware of the many metaphysical dimensions on planet Earth that continued to express elm tree energy—realms where vast, untouched forests still clothed the land. Trees, palms, and plants of a bygone age, long vanished from the physical three-dimensional Earth, all thrived and grew, along with plants of the present and even the future, for life is an undeniable, ongoing continuity, regardless of the drama being acted out on a physical planet, Earth.

Gradually, my focus as Elm became centered on a small garden in the English countryside of planet Earth. In the spherical time of Elm consciousness, no time had passed. Within Elm consciousness, no drama existed, for Elm related to life through consciousness, and its tree form merely expressed this consciousness in a physical reality. Elm's metaphysical reality endured, no matter what befell the physical. However, I was aware that over a century had passed since the last Elm had died, yet, wonder of wonders, a strong healthy elm flourished and grew no more than a mile from where the last Elm had died.

Once again I faced the paradox of time and Oneness. How could another elm exist when the last Elm had died? But in the timeless frame of consciousness, the answer was apparent. With the last Elm dead, all trace of the killer elm disease also died. In consciousness, the energy of Elm was held, anchored and nourished by every elm in every other time-frame reality, while in linear time about twenty-five cleansing years passed. When I made the discovery of another thriving elm, Elm consciousness had already refocused its energy into the newborn seedling. I realized that just as I had earlier backtracked across an illusory—yet real!—linear time frame to teach farmer-me, so Elm consciousness could refocus into any time frame that was appropriate to its continuity, manifesting an endless thread of connection that transcended time, space, and form.

While sharing the consciousness of Elm, I had perceived time frames of far-distant futures and long-ago pasts—all held in the Now—experiencing the connection of a greater reality, when, with Elm, I settled into the valley of a totally different environment on a very distant planet. Other vegetation grew in forms unfamiliar to me, yet I recognized the consciousness of many extinct Earth plants. Elm now grew flat and saucerlike, about a kilometer in diameter, with tissue-thin leaves forming a vast rosette of the palest blue. The atmosphere would have been unbreathable for humanity, although other creatures abounded here. I was aware of some small Beings who were caretakers of the plant that Elm had been drawn to for its new expression of consciousness. As a result of the supposed tragedy of its apparent death on Earth, Elm now flourished again as a new expression began its evolution elsewhere. I was aware that this new evolution could only begin when the last Elm on Earth withdrew. Unlike humanity of Earth, the Beings of the other planet were fully aware of the One in the consciousness of all plants and all creatures, and through Nature, they enjoyed a heightened synthesis unknown to humanity.

I marveled at the intelligence and purpose behind the movement of consciousness and its physical vehicle. With a new projection of consciousness commencing, Elm transcended time to continue its Earth-form evolution.

How had Elm survived on Earth? I viewed the answer from Elm consciousness, for a single, unrealized connection had remained. When the group of people walked away from Elm, unsure of how they would save the magnificent tree, Faye had lingered for a few moments. She had scooped up a handful of the biomass beneath Elm and had noticed a single flat, winged seed. Slipping the seed into her pocket, she had hurried to catch up with the others.

Many years had passed, and Faye's old coat had been discarded to hang on a peg in her closet. Years later, now married and on a visit home for a respite from her young children, Faye had found the coat, and the associated memories of the last Elm had brought tears to her eyes. Idly, her fingers went through the pockets of the old coat, where they touched upon the seed of Elm. For a second she felt a breathless excitement as she held the seed before her; then the excitement died. Seldom did the seed of an English elm grow, for it was mostly barren. The tree was generally propagated by suckers, and of course, they were all long gone. But as Faye held the seed, a feeling entered her heart that this special seed contained life—a strong undeniable intuition that regenerated her excitement.

Watched by her father, Gus, Faye set the tree seed at the bottom of his garden, not far from the site of the last Elm. Gus was convinced that it was all a waste of time, for with barren seed and the passing of years, what chance the Elm? However, he promised to water the seed and to care for it, for, deep down, he wanted to believe in miracles.

A month before the poison had been fed into its roots, Elm had dropped its seed. In only a very few, a tiny reservoir of energy held Elm consciousness, and since Elm had died, all but one of these flickering sparks had expired. In the miracle of Nature, a single tiny seed held all the consciousness of the eventual massive tree that it would one day become, for Nature deals not in the size of form but in the essence of life.

It was this single living seed that Faye reverently kissed and planted in her father's garden.

When, after three anxious months, Elm's strong green shoot emerged from the soil, Gus unashamedly knelt down next to it and bawled like a child, tears streaming down his cheeks.

"It's a miracle," he whispered. "A bloody miracle."

Elm became known as Faye's Elm, and no tree ever received more protection or love than Faye's Elm.

I watched the story of Elm continue, the repercussions of its resurrection once again affecting the lives of those who had been involved in the final drama. New players entered as Elm grew.

Of all this, only one more thread need be followed. Not unnaturally, this thread involved Faye, for with the growth of her Elm, a bonding in consciousness took place.

Faye and her family moved back into the village of her childhood, and she spent many hours each week simply sitting in silence with her tree. She learned a truth that she spoke about to conservation groups and wrote about for all who were interested. She learned by *direct knowing*— by realizing that she could merge the focus that was her conscious Self with the consciousness of Elm. In this way, she had access to the wisdom and intelligence of the Beingness of Elm. The truth that she came across was based in the continuity of All Life.

Faye learned that if we are to save the trees on Earth, all people involved must become aware of their inner feelings. Are they Fayes or Billys? If a group of people fight to save some trees and their fighting is based on fear — a fear for the survival of the planet and their children — then whether the trees are saved or not is irrelevant. No matter how noble the motive, fear is not the basis of unity. Fear-based actions threaten the extinction of many species of trees, yet if the defense of the trees is also based on fear, in consciousness nothing creative happens. Fear is a force of restriction, of separation. If a thousand fearful people plant a thousand trees a day, then fear plants the trees, and fear will just as surely remove them. In a year or a hundred years, a fear-based action will reap the harvest of separation and more fear.

If, however, a person plants a single tree each month, or each week or each year, and planting that tree is a pure expression of that person's love, with no motive other than the joy of sharing life with that tree, then in consciousness this act will affect the entire universe — and Beyond. Love connects and creates. Saving trees is not a numbers' game, because numbers become meaningless in the reality of One. Oneness means that the One is not the sum total of its parts; it means that the One has never been divided. In truth, a forest is not just a large number of separate trees creating an ecological diversity; it is also the consciousness of One seeking to express Oneness through the diversity of species. Saving trees on our physical Earth

38

depends entirely on the relationship we create with them and the development of that relationship. If we grow in consciousness as the trees grow in stature, then we have the potential to affect the substance and structure of the future of all life on Earth.

All this and more, Faye learned from the reservoir of Elm wisdom with which she had bonded. In her loving relationship with Elm, she, too, became a pivot for change in the development of human consciousness.

As I soared across the All That Is, releasing the consciousness of Elm, one more truth became apparent to Faye; no misaction or misdeed is wasted by consciousness, not even the death of the last Elm on Earth!

☀

I stood before the mural, my outstretched hand reaching toward a branch of Elm.

"Incredible," I murmured, as my arm fell to my side.

"Quite an experience," Seine said, his words soundless but clear in my head. He smiled his inscrutable smile. "What did you learn from it?"

"Don't you know what happened?" I asked.

Seine had no eyelids, but his eyes were able to widen into greater orbs of silver or to become mere slits. Each expression carried volumes of communication. Right now, his eyes were large, round, and innocent.

"I know to a certain extent, for as your guide I share a synthesis with you within consciousness. This excludes any possibility of inadvertent misunderstanding in our relationship. A necessity, I'm sure you will agree. But I do not intrude on your inner privacy. I would like you to share this with me."

"I learned a lot about elm trees," I said playfully, "and through Elm I learned a lot about *all* trees."

"Please continue," Seine said, his eyes and tone becoming more serious.

"More than anything, I learned that we need to *honor* Nature. Trying to *save* Nature is based on fear and illusion but to *honor* it is based in truth. The difference is not in our actions, but in a redirection of our focus and consciousness as we act."

I paused, pacing up and down in front of the mural, aware now that an occasional breeze was moving the leaves of Elm. "So much happened in the experience that I hardly know how to continue," I said as I paced. "However, looking at the areas of impact, the most important would have to be the connectedness of Nature. While I have long realized that human reality is overwhelmed by the illusion of separation, this is not so in the kingdoms of Nature. Nature has not the vaguest concept of separation. Not the minerals or the plants or any of the animals. The reality of Nature is the connection and wholeness of All Life. The grain of sand knows only a total connectedness with the planet Earth; it knows nothing of isolation or of being lesser or greater than a mountain of rock or a nugget of gold."

I felt surprised, for as I shared my insight, it continued to grow and expand. "I learned that Nature has no relationship with separation. In other words, a hundred thousand elm trees are not a hundred thousand separate trees;

they are the multiple expression of the consciousness of
Elm. Not a single elm has any perception of being isolated
in its distance from another elm, whether that may be a
few meters or many thousands of kilometers. Elm consciousness is One. You cannot affect one elm tree without affecting all elm trees. When elm disease began to
destroy a few, it weakened the many. Equally, if a huge
swarm of a species of leaf-eating insect attacked a number of elms, and the trees began to produce a poison in
their sap to counter the attack, that sap would also be
produced by elm trees far away from the attack. Amazingly, it would be strongest in the elm closest to the attack, becoming less and less toxic at greater distances away.
This would seem to indicate that the trees recognize distance and therefore separation, but that is not so. I learned
that in the consciousness of Elm, a certain intensity of discord evokes an equally proportionate countermeasure to
bring about balance. Balance is the factor that determines
the intensity of response to the attack, localizing it in consciousness. Of course, as it is with Elm, so it is with all
species of trees and plants."

Seine had moved away from the mural, and as I finished
speaking, I was facing him. I paused in my pacings, surprised at the extent of my insight.

Seine's eyes were wide, round, and luminous, his whole
expression one of approval, yet he was staring at the mural
behind me as though he had not seen it before.

I spun around . . . and gasped. The Elm and copse of
trees had gone, to be replaced by a beautiful English Park.
Before me was an extensive area of mowed grass, dotted

with large, mature trees. A huge oak caught my eye, its branches gnarled with the majesty of age, while nearby stood several horse chestnuts and a lone sycamore, similar to one I used to climb as a boy. Everywhere was green — green as only the English countryside can be in early summer. In the foreground, a row of tall, narrow poplar trees, with a footpath along their left side, seemed to fade away into the distance.

"How did that happen?" I asked Seine.

"You are the creative influence here," he replied. "Why don't you go and find out what it means."

I frowned. "You mean enter the mural the way I did last time? But that just happened. I can't just walk in."

"Oh! You know that for a fact, do you?"

"So what do I do?" I asked in exasperation. "Just step into it like . . . this!" So saying, I took a step toward the footpath, . . .

✳

. . . and I was in the park, standing alongside the row of huge old poplars. "Ho hum," I muttered. "I've done it again. Now what?"

I waited awhile for either cosmic intervention or divine inspiration to make it all clear, but nothing happened. Meanwhile, the well-trodden dirt path seemed to beckon, so I strolled along it, walking past the regularly spaced and massive poplar trees.

A sycamore, evoking memories of my past, invited me with mute but eloquent limbs to recapture my boyhood in its network of branches, but I resisted. Instead, I followed the footpath. After walking some way, I got the strange impression that a Roman soldier stood in the trunk of each tree, somehow encased, yet when I stopped to look directly, I was simply gazing at a huge single tree. Nevertheless, as I strolled on, the impression remained.

Most odd, I thought, but then, everything about this expanded reality is odd when compared with normal standards. Eventually, I reached the end of the long row of poplars, and following the curve of the footpath, I found that it passed under an obviously old, yet very impressive, yew tree. It was the biggest specimen I had ever seen. Beneath it was a simple wooden bench seat.

The bench faced away from me, and I saw that it had an occupant. As I drew close, with a shock, I realized it was Treenie.

"My God! What are you doing here?" I exclaimed, as I hugged and kissed her.

"Waiting for you," she smiled.

"What? How come I'm the one who never quite seems to know what's going on until I'm right in the middle of it?"

"That's a good question," she laughed. "Probably because you are a bit more reluctant than most."

I looked at her appraisingly. "The fact that you are here indicates that you are also involved with Seine. I assume you know him?"

"Of course. For a *very* long time."

I asked Treenie how she got here and a dozen other similar trite questions, and she answered them about as well as I would if someone had asked me, so I gave up the idle chatter and decided to get to the point of the exercise.

"Okay, my love, why am I here?"

"What were your impressions as you walked along the footpath?" she asked me.

"I fail to see what that has to do with why I am in this Park," I countered.

She gave me her "Oh dear, are you going to be difficult?" look, so I stopped being evasive.

"Okay, okay. I felt a strong desire to climb a large familiar sycamore tree, a kind of 'rekindling' of my youth, but I decided to 'leaf' it alone," I said, grinning at my puns.

Treenie just gazed at me patiently, never overly enthusiastic about my wit. She sighed.

"Apart from that, the only other strong impression was really quite odd. I had the feeling that there was a Roman soldier encased in the trunk of each poplar tree, but when I looked directly at the trunk, there was nothing but the tree."

Treenie smiled at me. "I knew you would see them; that's why I'm here. The soldiers you perceived were killed in battle a long time ago. Because they died under very honorable circumstances, they were buried here as a tribute to their bravery. On each grave, a tiny poplar seedling was planted. However, these soldiers had been part of a fighting unit since they were young boys, training and growing to manhood together. They were encouraged to be a unit, not thinking individuals, and this was so deeply impressed into their subconscious that when death swept them up, they were unprepared. Even in death they clung to their established group identity. They were too conditioned and fearful to depart to their separate destinies."

"What happened to them?" I interjected.

Treenie frowned at me. "Each bewildered soul identified with the poplar tree on his grave. They thereby clung once more to a type of group expression and locked themselves into a limbo of man/tree group identity. They are absolutely incapable of releasing themselves. So, my darling, that is your task."

I sat astonished for a few moments. "What am I supposed to do? And why me?"

"If, as I assume it to be, the timing is right, you will know how and why. Michael, just do it."

Feeling puzzled, I got up from the bench and walked back to the row of poplars. If I was going to get any divine inspiration, I certainly needed it now and quickly, because I had no idea what to do.

As I reached the first poplar, I faced it. Instantly, I had a *knowing* that there were exactly one hundred trees, and that a whole legion of one hundred centurions had been buried here. For long, timeless moments, I just stood there, hoping that feelings of love and compassion would arise in me, but they did not. Apart from some sympathy, I felt nothing. Did I really care? I thought about the soldiers and about the faithful service they had given, only to die, forgotten. Did anybody care? Who even knew why they died? What difference had it made to history? Was it even recorded? I thought of them lying in these lonely graves. What did it really mean to grow up from boyhood trained to fight and kill? Had they laughed and had real fun? Had they ever been really loved by women, beyond casual sex? Had they been no more than trained killing machines, maybe not even knowing what they were fighting for? Was killing other soldiers their ultimate goal in life? Had they been emotionally crippled, deliberately suppressing all their finer feelings and values? What a tragic, empty, meaningless life.

Only then did an unexpected wave of love for these poor, lost souls surge through me. I cared. I felt a real depth of compassion. With these strong feelings, a light seemed to form around me, flickering and growing as I focused not on the soldiers, but on the love. Gradually, the light grew until it was a strong radiance emanating from me, bathing the trunk of the poplar tree that I faced in its white light.

As I watched, the Roman soldier slowly was revealed in the trunk of the tree. He was both separate and fully contained. I watched him pass through stages of dread and fear, his mouth opening in a silent scream as he struggled to stay hidden in the tree, but the light relentlessly exposed him. I saw his gradual dawning of comprehension as the light permeated him, and the wild hope that crossed his face as he heard my words.

"You are now free. Step to my side."

For moments longer he struggled, part of him trying to shrink back into the tree, while another part longed to be free; then, slowly, hesitantly, he stepped away from the tree, staggering slightly, before coming upright, straight and proud. His eyes met mine in wonder and recognition.

Together, we walked to the next tree, and I repeated

the same process, except this time I experienced even more love and a greater radiance of light. Again, after some faltering hesitation, the soldier stepped away from the tree and into formation. Thus we went on, from tree to tree. By the twelfth tree, the radiance that surrounded us was so powerful, no words were needed. We were able to move along at a slow march, each soldier stepping away from his tree and into rank behind me.

Once again, I was filled with *knowing*; these were my own legionnaires. I had been the centurion general. Who else but I should free these men? We continued the slow march until we reached the last tree and released the last soldier. I turned and faced the legion, men with whom I had fought and died. To a man, we had all been killed.

As I gazed at these men, into eyes fastened hungrily on mine—eyes filled with complete trust—the light grew in volume and intensity until it began to consume them. I watched as the soldiers gradually dissolved into this incredible light, each soul moving at last to its own destiny. Soon, I stood alone.

With their release, the light faded until it was no more than an ethereal glow around me. As I walked back down the row of huge poplars toward the yew tree, I knew that their life energy had also fled. Even the poplars had been locked by the human souls into a cycle far longer than their natural allotted life span. Already, their leaves were turning yellow, falling softly to the ground. Before long, they would be cut down and removed, for I knew that this Park was real and that this experience was also embedded in a linear-time reality.

Treenie was waiting on the bench. "You see, my darling, I knew you could do it."

Sitting next to her I gave her a hug. "I learned that I died also. What happened to me?"

"You were ever an independent spirit, so you were not locked in with your soldiers. In a way, I suppose you deserted them in death. Now you have released them."

"Yes, but what happened to my body?"

"You were buried with your men, right here. You have always admired the long-lived evergreen yew tree, so I planted it on your grave."

"You!" I leapt to my feet. "But . . . "

"There really is no need to shout Michael," Seine said quietly.

I was standing once more in the Temple of Learning before the mural of a Park in the English countryside. I stared. It was early summer, but the row of poplars was now almost bare of leaves.

3

Regarding Reluctance

It is not the love of angels that will uplift humanity;
it is our ability to truly love one another and ourselves.

"That was most remarkable. I still don't know how Treenie got there."

"Do you know how you got there?" Seine asked.

I laughed. "No, I don't. So if I don't know how I got there, it's pointless trying to understand how Treenie did."

"Something like that," Seine replied. "Understanding is not always appropriate, for it attempts to rationalize mystery. Mystery is truth unrealized, while most understanding is based on rationalization rather than realization."

As he glanced at me, Seine's eyes again became disconcerting slits of silver. "Please follow me."

With a mixed feeling of trepidation and puzzlement, I followed Seine as he preceded me through another vaulted archway into a different wing of the Temple of Learning. From the outer appearance, all this inner space was impossible, but this was a reality that seemed to specialize in impossible possibilities!

Apart from a glow of soft white translucence, there was nothing in this part of the building. Every part of it glowed— floor, walls, and the ceiling far above. This created an atmosphere of tranquillity, which was probably exactly what Seine desired.

"You can sit and relax here if you wish."

I looked at the space indicated. "You mean on the floor? There aren't any seats." I felt foolish stating the obvious.

Chuckling, Seine leaned back, swung his long, furry legs off the floor, and, somehow suspended, relaxed.

"Try it."

Very cautiously, I leaned back, and to my surprise, I felt an incredibly comfortable, yielding firmness supporting my body, perfectly contoured to me. Still cautious, I relaxed into it, trying to see what it was. There was nothing, not even a blur of light.

"This is great."

"Glad you like it. It will also nourish you."

Even as Seine spoke his silent words, I could feel vitality surging through me like a small, soft wave. Seine looked at me, his silver eyes willing my gaze to meet his, yet not compelling it.

"What do you want?" I asked.

"Don't play games, Michael. You know perfectly well what I want from you. I want your intentions clarified."

I did know. The issue was my reluctance. Reluctance seemed to be part of my life. I had been reluctant to be born to another Earth cycle, and very reluctant about my schooling. However, I *had* been very keen to marry Treenie! Reluctance never stopped me from doing things; it created an obstacle I had to overcome — me! I seldom spoke of this reluctance, but I knew Treenie was acutely aware of it. However, on the bright side, anything to do with Nature found a natural bypass. The real crux of the matter was that I had no desire to speak in public. Paradoxically, I had

51

learned that becoming free is the birth of purpose, and I knew that my purpose entailed sharing my vision of truth with both written and spoken words. My reluctance and my purpose were at odds! However, in keeping with my purpose, I was now involved in public speaking, albeit a mite reluctantly!

These were the thoughts I deliberately projected and shared with Seine.

"So where do I go from here?" I asked. "I can't deny my reluctance or pretend I don't feel it. For all that I am, and do, enthusiasm abounds, especially about writing about my experiences, but the speaking seems pointless. As for my intentions, I'm continually looking for ways to say what needs to be said in the most acceptable and appropriate way. I intend to follow my purpose, but I need to feel that it's not a purposeless exercise."

Seine looked at me with an expression of great concern.

"How about love?" he asked.

"Seine, that's fine, but how do I offer it? With more words? People today are consumed by the problems associated with day-to-day living. The bills to be paid; the problems with kids; the rape, incest, and drugs; trying to keep a relationship together and make a living; and on and on. That's what's referred to as the real world. The fact that this real world is based on the untruth of separation makes no difference to them. At this moment, it's *their* truth. For the majority of people, this stew pot of complexity is their reality."

Seine still looked concerned, but when he spoke, I realized that the concern was not for me.

"A brilliant summary. It should go a long way toward maintaining your reluctance."

"That's a bit unfair."

Seine's eyes were sparkling slits. "While I deny nothing that you have said, yet it cannot be an excuse. You realize this, don't you?"

Reluctantly, I nodded my acquiescence.

"Any more words I add to this discussion are unlikely to affect the issue," Seine said thoughtfully.

He slid effortlessly out of the invisible force field in which he had been lounging. "Wait here for a while," he said, and he walked away across the temple and was out of sight almost instantly.

I felt uneasy. Knowing Seine the way I did, his dismissal of my reluctance was very much out of character. I had a feeling that he was allowing other forces to become involved, but what were they? Surely I was safe in a room of nothing but softly illumined walls. I was lost in a thoughtful reverie, trying in vain to find a solution that would free me from my reluctance, when I suddenly noticed a small boy approaching me.

He reached me as I struggled my way out of the nonphysical recliner. I knelt down to be on a level with him.

"Who are you?" I asked.

"I am Thane."

"Thane? That's an odd sort of name. Does it have a meaning?" I asked him.

"In normal terms of reference, it relates to the warrior companion of a Scottish king, but there is a higher meaning."

He was silent for so long I prompted him. "Such as?"

His dark eyes held mine, transfixing me. He said nothing, just gave me that knowing stare, as though waiting for recognition. Recognition! He looked as I had at about six years of age. The only difference was I had been fair-haired and blue-eyed. His hair and eyes were as black as night. As I gazed at him, my eyes moistened, even though I was not in a physical reality, and a tear trickled down one cheek. An immensity of love swelled in my heart, yet recognition hovered too far away to be captured.

"I . . . I know you, yet I don't."

"Thane also means a disciple of truth," he told me.

I felt that a hand was squeezing my heart, and I was choking as my throat became thick. I recognized him, and in the recognition, my emotions ran wild.

He smiled now, with compassion and ageless wisdom. "I am an aspect of Self that has never physically incarnated and never will. You and I are not really you and I at all; we are One. We are a disciple of truth."

He paused and waited while my emotions gradually subsided. Finally, all that remained was love, for love is not an emotion. I could not understand why he appeared to me as a child, but it seemed unimportant.

He continued. "You have met and merged with many of your human identities of incarnation, resolving your past conflict. Reluctance remains. We are One, so I understand at least an aspect of your dilemma. Because you now perceive the perfection of the world, nothing that you say or do can improve or reduce that perfection. The experience of truth means you can speak of nothing less than truth. Those who experience that truth do not need to be told, while those who do not would say that you are totally deluded. Does that summarize it?"

I nodded.

"Michael, I have one question for you. If the flowers of Earth did not get pollinated, would the plants that depend on pollination continue to flower?"

The answer was obvious. "Of course not. Only the mature plants could carry on flowering each year, but no new plants could be propagated from seed. Eventually, the plants would all die."

"And would that also be perfect?"

I felt shocked by this powerfully graphic question.

"Pollinate the flowers of humanity with truth," Thane continued, "for the seeds of a new and expanded reality are greatly needed in your world."

Hesitantly, I confessed to a deep inner concern. "I often question whether I have enough love and compassion to do what is needed. When I believed in the illusion of separation, I had a fierce desire to change the world, but that desire was based on self-deceit and fear. Now that I relate to a greater truth, I have no desire to change anything. Perhaps I don't care enough. Maybe that is the truth of my reluctance."

His black eyes regarded me solemnly. "As an aspect of Self, I know better. Did you not feel compassion for the Roman soldiers? Have you not wept for humanity?"

"Yes, but I was slow to respond."

"And is it wrong if your deeper feelings are not immediately on the surface?"

I said nothing.

"Do you remember the metaphysical incident that happened when you were seventeen years old?" Thane asked. "It involved a family in a slum."

"That was a dream," I said defensively.

"You *know* it was not. That was your way of dealing with it. Do you really believe that all that happened was that you went to sleep with a stack of books on your lap while sitting in the public library at Cambridge? You even have difficulty cat-napping on a bed during the day! No, Michael, the timing was perfect. It was a moment of receptivity and openness. At that moment in the library, when you stepped out of the physical and into your light body, you were more awake than you had been in a long time."

I remembered it clearly. I had been reading about the love and compassion of a relatively obscure doctor in the nineteenth century and of the personal sacrifices he had made in the execution of his duty—a duty based on love. I had felt deeply moved and inspired. For long moments I had felt an inner shift, as though I hovered in some other space, and then the experience that I had designated as a daydream took place.

Thane smiled. "But you were reluctant! You remember the struggle with your compassion, and how you tried to negate the experience. However, despite yourself, you did express your love and caring."

"How do you know all this?"

"Do you remember the angel?"

"Yes, of course."

"That was me."

"Oh my God!" The memory of the experience hit me

like a shock wave. Even as I collapsed limply back into the invisible recliner, I was swept up by the incident as it once again became my reality.

✳

I was staring at a dim and dingy house in a squalid slum. Dirty paper and refuse littered the steps leading up to the backdoor of the scruffiest looking house I had ever seen. Despite feeling repelled and threatened by this strange vision in the public library, I experienced my light-body self getting up from the chair, walking over to the house, and starting up the steps. In my physical consciousness, I balked at what was happening, but my light-body self continued that grim ascent with unassailable determination.

I climbed a long flight of iron steps, leading from the back of an alley. Although it was daytime, light was sparse in a street where the sun scarcely ever penetrated—a street narrow with despair and ruin. Paint flaked from the shaky handrail, and everything I touched was gritty with dirt. My actions were compelled by my light-body self, so despite my distaste, I opened the battered door and walked in. If the door looked as though it had been kicked to death, the interior of the house looked even more savagely mauled. I stared around, aghast. This was the opposite of all the order and cleanliness in my own life. Pots and pans, grimy with fat and old food, lay in a heap in a corner, while a filthy table with two chairs occupied the center of the room. A sofa, looking as though it had been resurrected from a rubbish dump, angled along a wall, one leg missing. Blistered paint peeled from huge damp patches on walls and ceilings, showing scarcely a trace of its original color. The place reeked of mold, damp filth, tobacco smoke, and, overpowering it all, beer.

I stared around me, appalled. Somewhere an urgent thought was trying to surface—Get out, quick!—but an inner commitment held me. It was the people in the room who triggered the urge to run. In one of the chairs, a man lay with his head and torso slumped onto the table. A dirty, limp hand clutched an empty beer bottle, while the man cradled his head on the other arm. His eyes were closed, and spittle drooled from his slack lips. Three or four days' growth of beard had formed a gray cloud around his face, and a lone fly walked unconcerned across his bald head. Completing this picture of degenerate squalor was a stained and soiled shirt stretched tight over a bulging beer gut, partly tucked into a pair of tattered trousers. This man epitomized everything I most despised in humanity.

He was not alone. Stretched out on the sofa, a blowsy, peroxide blond, complete with garish red lipstick, snored in a soft, gurgling monotone. Her face was slack and some-how empty, as though all pride and self-respect had long been eroded. With a once white blouse draped over a stained and rumpled black skirt, she was unkempt and slut-tish. A movement caught my eye. Sitting in the ashes of an empty fireplace, a thin dirty boy poked listlessly with a stick at some charred wood. I walked over to him and knelt down, staring in shock. He was maybe eighteen months to two years old, and his face was pinched in around the cheeks, his eyes watery and scabby. There were no marks of violence on him, but neglect had stamped despair and defeat onto a face made old, tragically replacing the bloom of love and nourishment. The vest he wore was his only clothing, while around his genitals he was chapped red, filthy, and scabby. And he stank. The acrid smell of vomit and feces hovered around him, attracting a buzzing swarm of houseflies.

I stood up, nauseated and disgusted. For long moments, a fury grew in me, threatening to burst out, but in this light-body self, it was impossible. The physical, personal me would have left or would have abused the man and woman verbally—no, the personal me would never have become involved—but this was another aspect of me, in a place and situation that I *knew* existed and was actually happening.

Why am I here? I pleaded silently. What am I supposed to do? What do I have to learn? How can I help? As clearly as the sound of a chiming bell, an angelic voice spoke into my mind. With the sound of the voice, I saw a Being of Light, just as I had imagined an angel would look, minus the wings. It was human in configuration, small, and somehow illumined from within, so I was unable to see any features. I was disconcerted rather than surprised, for the Being radiated an overwhelming essence of purity. Questions rushed into my mind, but I lost the initiative as the Light Being spoke its own question first.

"Why do you feel such revulsion for these people?"

Despite being rather surprised by the insight that the question implied, I answered truthfully.

"Because they represent everything I despise in humanity," I answered in my thoughts.

"Do you forget that they are human, just as you are?"

"Of course I don't. But they didn't have to get in this pathetic and disgusting state."

"So you have judged them and found them guilty?"

"That's unfair. *They* created the squalor they are in. Nobody else did it to them. I can see the evidence, so it's not a matter of judging."

"I do not deny what you see. I ask you to question what you cannot see."

I was feeling a bit nonplussed. "Why criticize me? After all, I'm not the guilty party here."

"You see. You have found them guilty."

"You're confusing me. What's the point of all this?"

"Compassion. Compassion instead of condemnation."

I was feeling even more confused. "I can't help what I feel, can I? They violate everything about decency that I believe in."

"You are saying, then, that *you* are the victim of your feelings and your beliefs. Is it not possible that these people could make the same claim?"

Now I was angry. "Look! What's the purpose behind all this, apart from trying to trick me with words?"

"I'm not tricking you with words. I'm simply reflecting them back for you to reconsider. That alone is purpose enough."

"Okay! Suppose I accept that. Suppose I concede that I have been inadvertently judging these people. How does that help change anything?"

"You can only bring real change into a situation if *you* also are prepared to change."

"But I don't need to change! Oh! You mean, can I find compassion in me rather than disgust?"

"Would that not be a powerful change?"

"Yes, I guess it would." With that realization came a feeling of humiliation. "But what *is* compassion? I'm ashamed to confess I don't exactly know what it is!"

"You certainly do. You felt it as you read about the doctor. You are here, now, because you have chosen to make it a reality in your life. By being compassionate, you will acknowledge and accept it rather than continue to deny it."

I was surprised. "Do you know all about me?"

"Of course."

"Are you my guardian angel?"

"*Guiding* angel would be a better term."

"Well, why didn't you say so?"

"Does it make any difference? You only hear me when you allow it. I speak wisdom as a whisper, while your own fear and foolishness shout at you. Will you listen now?"

"Of course I will."

"Give your attention to the people in this room. See if you can find love for them within your heart."

I walked over to the man, trying to feel some sort of sympathy for him. I felt nothing—no stirring of sympathy, love, or compassion—nothing but disgust. I looked at the snoring woman, feeling loathing rather than love.

"I'm afraid I'm not too good at this," I said. I then turned my attention to the little boy. Concern and sympathy flared like a match within me. I knelt next to him, wanting to pick him up, but I could not. Physically, I was not there. I saw lice crawling through the hair on his head, and I felt misery rolling off him in waves of despair. I wanted to hug and comfort him.

"I do care. I want nothing more than to help this poor boy, although his parents can go to hell. Look what they've done to him."

"So you feel a spark of limited love but also unforgiveness and even hate. Is this the best you can manage? Do you not yet realize that it is not age that determines who is the child in this room?"

I felt criticized and reactive. "What's all this about? What difference does it make whether I love them or not?"

"If you can love them, accepting them just as they are, this love becomes a light in their darkness, a door opening where all others are closed. It allows and encourages the formation of their own self-respect, moving them from hopelessness to hope. Both of these people are consumed by self-loathing, by self-disgust. Do you think they need more of this? They are in this situation now because they cannot face themselves. They need to be loved for who they are, not for what they could be under different circumstances."

"If you know so much and you're so good at loving, why don't you love them? Obviously you're better at it than I am," I said defiantly.

"Alas, it is not the love of angels that will uplift humanity; it is the love of each of you, one for another, and for all. And even more than this, love for yourselves. This is the great lesson of humanity."

I knew, despite my reluctance, that I was facing a challenge that would carry its repercussions throughout my life. Maybe even more so than for the people in this room.

Knowing that I could not force love, I squatted on the floor next to the boy, focusing on him. I allowed an empathy to build between us, connecting and uniting us. Gradually, I felt something from deep inside me reaching out to embrace the little boy, gathering him to me. Only then did I notice that he and I were surrounded by Light, a Light growing steadily stronger. Slowly, somehow controlled by me in a way I did not comprehend, the Love-Light spread through the room, until it encompassed both the man and woman in its aura. With a sense of awe, I realized that I *did* care about the parents—I cared very much—but my caring came from so deeply within me that I had not known such feelings existed.

As my acceptance of the family surfaced into my awareness, so the Love-Light increased in power. Then something happened. The woman opened her eyes and stared at the child. An expression of self-disgust crossed her features, and shaking her head in pity, she got off the sofa and stumbled across the room. She couldn't see me, the angel, or the Love-Light. Picking up the little boy, she kissed him on his forehead, her eyes widening as she glimpsed the lice crawling over his scalp.

Her words were a cry of despair. "Oh Christ, Bill, we can't do this to the kid. What the hell are we doing to ourselves, to all of us?"

With a groan, Bill sat up. "What's up? What'd you say?"

"I said we've got to get out of the mess we're in. We've got a kid crawling with lice, while we're both stinking with booze. Christ, Bill! We can't go on like this. What the hell has happened to us?"

Guilt creased Bill's face as he stared at the boy. "I don't know," he muttered. "Can't get work."

"Yeah, you can't get work, but do we have to live like pigs? Christ! It's like I've never seen this room before. It stinks, and so do you . . . and me." She began to cry, shame and sorrow etched into her eyes.

The angel turned toward me, its light flickering with tints of gold. "The healing has begun. You were the agent for change because you also embraced change, even if in a limited way. As you surmised, the situation is real, and for this family, their deepest despair is ended. With help from other people, they will repair their lives."

I felt pleased with what was happening, but the comment about my limited change jarred in me. "What's so limited about my own change? That's a real put-down."

The angelic energy was directed straight at me. "You think so? Look at these people, and feel your love now."

I looked at the family as they stirred from their drink-sodden apathy—and stared in shock. Suddenly, the man had *my* face, as did the woman and boy! They *all* had my face. I recoiled in repugnance, and the Love-Light abruptly dimmed.

"You see! You can find some love for them, but if I show you yourself in them, you are again repulsed."

"But . . . but . . . but . . . " I spluttered helplessly.

"But you must embrace in yourself what you can embrace in others. You condemn in yourself what the drunken man symbolizes. He is that part of you that is frequently

64

out of control, the self-pitying aspect that sees yourself as unworthy. Love for yourself is the cure. The woman is your femininity, not necessarily beautiful in the way you equate with girls and beauty. Your feminine self is sensitive to the ugliness, but does not condemn it. Love your feminine self, not a fabrication of glamour. And the child is the child in you, neglected in the race to be an adult. Revive and revere the innocence and self-acceptance of the child. Do it by loving the child in you—the child as it is, not as you think it should be."

The silent words echoed and increased in intensity as though designed to be forever imprinted in my psyche, and the angelic light flared into a brilliance that jerked open my eyes as my head ducked away. I was sitting in the library, a bright shaft of sun from a high, narrow window hitting onto my face.

Badly shaken, I sat for a while simply digesting all that had taken place. The library was unfailingly the same library I visited regularly, yet I acknowledged that in some way unknown to me the paths of extended realities had met and merged. I did not like what had taken place. I found it extremely uncomfortable to consider the disgust I had felt at seeing my own face on those people in the slum. It was too painful to face the glaring truth of my lack of self-worth, so I buried it. Too much had been revealed for comfort. I forced the experience into a deep, dark place within, submerging it in that nether region where all my other nasty thoughts and feelings dwelt. Instead of embracing the capacity to examine myself honestly but without judgment, I dismissed it.

✳

With only the faintest sensation of displacement, I was back in the Temple of Learning, reclining in the invisible force-field seat.

Thane stared at me intently, a question in his eyes.

"Considering the circumstances and opportunity, that was not the smartest thing I ever did," I said flippantly. But I was shaken. How could I have been so dismissive of such an experience? So powerfully had I pushed it from me that only Thane, as a catalyst, had brought it back to my conscious awareness. It had emerged in my dreams quite regularly over the ensuing years, but the dreams, too, I had dismissed as nonsense.

"That is the potential value of dreams," Thane said, hearing my thoughts. "When people sleep, their consciousness can actively work toward their enlightenment, unhindered by the desires and wants that the mind is required to serve. Consciousness always seeks a higher purpose. However, do you still think that you lack the required compassion?"

I thought about it for a few moments, but I knew very clearly that I was a compassionate person. Perhaps I was not quickly ignited, but compassion was an inner force I could not deny.

Thane smiled. He knew!

4
Meadow of Eternity

As wisdom whispers its truth into your heart, accept it.
To empower this truth, live it.
In this way, you become illumined.

Thane spun gracefully on his heels and moved away. "Come on," he called. "I realize that a few buried memories need reviving. You cannot carry extra baggage on the journey you have undertaken. Come with me."

I could hardly believe how fast he was going—not in speed but in distance traveled. Seine moved in a similar fashion, somehow causing distance and placement to become altered.

I leapt out of the invisible recliner and hurried after Thane. Although he only appeared to be six years old, he was an aspect of Self that felt old and very wise.

"Wait," I called as he disappeared. I ran after him, chasing across the illumined room in an effort to catch up. I was skidding around a corner just as the thought entered my mind that perhaps he did not intend me to catch up, but by then it was too late.

I ran into a rubbish dump. I was about nine years old,

and I was in the rubbish dump just over the wall at the bottom of my parents' garden.

This dump was known as the Pit. The Pit was about three acres of household, shop, and warehouse rubbish. It was overrun and infested with rats, totally unsupervised and smelly, with an almost endless fire burning somewhere in its subterranean depths. Pretty good stuff for the gang of local kids that I mixed with.

I held the light, beautifully balanced Indian throwing spear that I used to hunt rats. Although I had a great love for Nature, my love affair ended with rats. I had a hatred of rats that began when one chewed its way into one of my rabbit hutches and ate most of the newborn babies. The big, old, scarred veteran rat was still crunching on its grizzly meal when I arrived at the hutches to see the babies early one morning. The mother rabbit, Jingo, was nearly frantic. I snatched open the hutch door and grabbed the rat as it tried to scramble through its hole in a corner. Frightened by what I was doing, I hung on even when the rat sank its teeth into my knuckle, before hurling it with a cry of rage against the brick wall. Two baby rabbits survived, but the loss of the others signaled the beginning of my war against rats, a vendetta that was to last several years.

The Pit became my hunting ground, and I became quite skillful with my throwing spear, many a rat kicking out its life on the sharp, flat blade.

Now, as I ran lightly across the wasteland toward the latest truckload of rubbish, I was eager to kill again. I slowed to a stalk. I knew exactly where the greatest concentration of rats was to be found. As dusk drew in, the truckloads of empty, five-pound jam tins, generally still containing great dollops of jam or marmalade, were a mecca for the rats, and Michael, the lone hunter, defender of mother rabbits and their babies, was there to destroy them. I stalked forward, my heart beating a furious rhythm as I spied the rats scurrying among the tins. Holding the spear at its point of balance, I drew back my arm, but everything went hazy.

I was under the shade of a tree in my Aunt Polly's large country garden. I was fourteen years old, and I was lazing in the rambling old garden, happy just being with Nature. The sun was hot, and the shade very welcome, so I sat for a while beneath the tree. But something odd happened. I was a fidgety, almost hyperactive boy, yet when I sat down, the deepest and most profound relaxation I had ever known seemed to overpower me. My eyes closed reluctantly but firmly. Around me, Aunt Polly's garden seemed to shimmer and melt, and strangely, through my closed eyelids, I could see a huge meadow filled with the largest, most beautiful buttercups I had ever seen. For a few moments, a thought struggled to be born—a vague thought about opening my eyes to reveal the lie of this inner vision— but it died unformed. The enchanting meadow beckoned with larger-than-life beauty, and I responded. Held in a relaxed state too deep to be disturbed, I became aware of myself as a body of light walking into the meadow, yet at the same time I was aware of the normal physical me sitting under the tree, still leaning against its trunk. For a brief, confused moment, I struggled with reality—which me was me?—but the deep relaxation held. Under its influence, insight suggested that each me was an aspect of my Self, and that I was simply dreaming while awake.

I walked deeper into the meadow, falling to my knees as I sniffed the great golden buttercups and gazed at the green splendor of the growth around me. I could smell the soil. I could even smell the collective plants, and it all seemed quite natural. Wild columbines and yellow-eyed daisies competed with my favorite cowslips for attention as I merged joyfully with Nature, abundant beyond anything I had ever dreamed. Before me, a stream trickled and gurgled its way under the caressing tickle of weeping willows and on through tall, bronze-headed bull rushes, while frogs and crickets sang a musical accompaniment to this enchanted wonderment.

When the first of the tiny threads of light appeared, it all seemed quite natural. Even when hundreds of them surrounded me, forming a circle of light rather like a living necklace of sparkling jewels, I felt no alarm. Rather, I felt a sense of recognition, as though this was no phenomenon at all, but a known reality sadly lacking in everyday life. Slowly, the living circle of light drew closer, until suddenly, I knew them as Nature Spirits. Where the knowing came from, I had no idea, but I knew it beyond all doubt. With this recognition, the tiny spirits closed the necklace of light until it touched me, and I was a golden buttercup, drinking in the sunlight as it played over my leaves with the touch of pure energy. Beings, far tinier than the threads

71

of light, lived within the cellular form of my buttercup self, weaving in an intricate and unending dance as they stitched the sun energy into the cells of my body.

From somewhere, silent words flowed from a vast, yet natural, source—a source I knew as the Spirit of Nature. Permeating all life on Earth, this ultimate wisdom whispered its truth into the buttercup self of me: *This imprint of your greater knowing will set you free. When that moment arrives, bursting through the illusions that bind you, your freedom will become a dedication to life. You will live to express that truth.* As those words flowed into me, I emerged from the buttercup, again a teenage boy in a body of light, continuing my journey along the edge of the stream.

Accompanied by the sparkling Nature Spirits, I entered a Nature that totally embraced me. Water voles sat up the better to see me, rather than slipping away with scarcely a ripple into the water, as was usual. They gazed at me, bright eyes black as berries, their whiskers twitching in curiosity.

"Do you see into this spectrum of light?" I whispered aloud, "How do you see me?"

Instantly, I was a water vole, my body a quivering mass of nervous energy as I watched the body of light regarding me from the other side of the stream. I was vole, and I was me! I was the totality of voleness, physically attuned to survival, yet also attuned to a spectrum beyond the intellect of humanity. I had thought that I could smell Nature when I first entered this wonderland, but now, as a water vole, I smelled all life. I could smell the movement in a rock, the ripples in the water. Smell functioned as sensory perception. I could even sense and define the intent of the boy of light across the stream from me. With this realization, I was again me, staring in humbled awe at the diminutive vole, seeing now its magnitude.

I had been able to sense my own intent—an intent based on love, admiration, and an overflowing wonder. In me, I had perceived curiosity, inquiry, and a deep appreciation for wildlife. I had smelled no vile stink filled with the intent to hurt or to kill, and I pondered on how I knew that there was a difference. Instantly, I experienced it. I was a rat, sitting on the water's edge, gnawing on a dead fish. I spied the boy at the same moment he spotted me, and I felt every hair on my body react to the stink and feel of anger that emanated from him. I had no way of knowing why he felt such loathing, but I was consumed by the quivering, snarling reaction of my senses. I wanted to run from the vileness, while equally I wanted to attack it, rending and destroying such an unnatural affliction.

I stared at the rat, feeling the outrage flush my body of light. For a few moments, the Spirits of Nature were diminished, the sparkles faltering; then they regained their light. A single thread flew to me, touching me between my eyes, and more powerfully than before, I felt the rat's experience of revulsion mix and merge with my own. I felt shame as I experienced how dirtied and sullied I was by my own emotions of hate for this creature.

"Why?" I whispered. "Why did you kill my baby rabbits?"

Hesitating, the rat stared at me, on the verge of scuttling away. As I stared back, the experience of rat became so powerfully my experience that my previous program of

73

hate was obliterated. In the consciousness of this young female rat, I saw an old rat, mean and cunning in the ways of their kind, gnaw and claw at the corner of my rabbit hutch until it could get in. I felt distress more acutely in the physical me under the tree than in my light-body self, for in becoming rat, I understood ratness. I understood that there was no malice in the rat as it killed the babies, ripping their bodies as it ate them while living. It was following its own nature. What I experienced was cruel, very cruel by human standards, but without malice. I *knew* then that Nature is without malice. I learned that malice was born and nurtured in humanity, and as I gazed at the rat self that I had become, I knew that it was my own malice that kept me hunting and killing rats in the Pit. What I most despised in the rat, I embodied. With this realization, shock flowed through each aspect of me, including the rat self. In the moment that I knew my obsession with killing rats had ended, so, as the young rat, I smelled the stink of my human intent go through a dramatic change; the stench of malice had vanished.

All ratness left me, and as a boy of light I followed the stream, captivated, as always, by the dance of moving water. I felt cleaner and more whole since my experience with the rat, and a deep inner gratitude washed over me. When I stopped to admire a great bronze dragonfly, I thrilled in expectation, but we remained separate within our connection. I felt a vast empathy with this beautiful insect. I wanted to fly as the dragonfly flew, and so great was my longing as it swept ahead of me up the stream that my body of light was suddenly flying without effort as I, too, swept along the surface of the water. Delight and surprise bubbled inside me, and I shouted my joy aloud, but the sound that emerged was a harsh "Keee Keeeee" as I flew up to perch on the swaying branch of a tree.

I watched the boy of light with bright-eyed interest, while he stood bewildered. I watched him look at his body, then up at me, and I felt his sense of awe as the total ending of separation overwhelmed him. He and I, boy and kingfisher, were One. For a brief instant, a flush of fear shook me—boy and kingfisher—then it was lost in wonder. There was no way to define when the merging ended. I simply became aware of myself as the boy of light, admiring the beauty of a kingfisher as it sat on a thin branch over the stream. But when it dived, exploding from the water with a tiny fish in its beak, I thrilled.

It seemed an eternity that I followed the stream as it meandered across an endless meadow. Time had no meaning. I was consumed in the experience of one after another of the creatures of the wild, and in each experience I became more whole in my relationship with Nature. Overlighting every moment, I felt some vast spiritual presence—an Intelligence of proportions beyond my ability to comprehend—and I was both mystified and comforted. I felt a promise moving from this great Spirit of Nature—a promise that one day this presence would become personified in my life, but the how and why remained a mystery.

While somewhere in the meadow of eternity, I felt a need to be physical again, yet with it came an immense sadness. I wanted to dwell in this enchanted state forever, a pupil of a mystical Nature, but my physical body pulled at me with an ache reminiscent of a headache. I lingered for a time, trying to deny my physical self, hiding beneath the bristling spines of a hedgehog. Again, my nose had the ability to put such a graphic form to the scents I inhaled that it enhanced my myopic eyesight. In each and every creature that I experienced, only this moment of life existed. Not a single shard of anxiety existed beyond the moment. If I was hunting for food, that was my totality. When I experienced the tingling rush and alarm of being hunted, the encoded genetic instincts of survival peculiar to the species dominated the moment totally. Even fear was a momentary thing, completely unlike human fear. It was fear, yet it was a mechanism based on life and living, not on death and dying or pain as in humanity. The difference was vast and inexplicable. Each moment of life was a totality of living, and I felt envy for such freedom. Nothing could convey this experience of Nature more profoundly than the absence of anxiety.

The insistent discomfort of physicality was too strong to deny. Reluctantly, I disconnected from hedgehogness and, in my light body, allowed the direction of return to be determined by my physical self. The threads of light accompanied me as I floated across the meadow, skimming over the grass and buttercups, yet all the while they were stitching invisible wisps of illumination into my psyche. Again, the silent words of the vast Spiritual Intelligence of Nature pervaded me. *As wisdom whispers its truth into your heart, accept it. To empower this truth, live it. In this way, you become illumined.*

My physical body shuddered as the wide-awake dream

ended. I opened my eyes, staring around me in shock. Normality was like returning to a twenty-watt gloom after the intensity of a thousand-watt light experience. After the incredible freedom I had known, I felt as though I were plunging into a dismal pit, isolated from Nature and life. Reality was again restricted and limited. The devastating sense of loss overwhelmed me, and I was crying before I knew it, my body shaking with grief. Even as I wept, a fear of the strangeness swept over me. I was at a loss for any kind of explanation; fearing for my sanity, I watched as one more metaphysical experience was buried in the murky depths of my subconsciousness. I rationalized the experience as a dream.

❊

"Oh!" I clapped my hands to my head as I skidded to a stop around a corner of the illumined room in the Temple of Learning.

Thane stood waiting for me. "I'm sorry," he said quietly, "but you had to take the experience in a rush. That way, you were involved before you could resist."

"I remember it all now, as clearly as though it were yesterday, yet I had forgotten. Any memory that strayed near the experience was dismissed as part of a daydream."

I stared at Thane intently. "The same Spirit of Nature guided me on my more recent journey into Nature. I wish I had been able to accept that earlier teenage experience."

"You had problems with acceptance and ridicule."

"I certainly did," I mused. "I obviously buried that mys-

77

tic experience very deeply. I could not talk to anyone about it. I knew at the time that the threads of light were fairies, but how do you talk about that when you are a fourteen-year-old boy in a very cynical world? I used to read about Noddy and Big Ears when I was a kid, but as a teenager such things were never talked about."

Thane's black eyes had a translucent quality as he looked at me. "When people do talk about the Spirits of Nature, or write stories for children, they inspire and ignite an inner dimension. Sometimes, unfortunately, they personalize the fairy folk far too much, giving them human characteristics. This has the effect of diluting their purity to the reader, and children grow away from them, finally labeling anything unbelievable a fairy story. This, in turn, isolates you from the mystical Spirits of Nature — Spirits you have labeled fairies, elves, and gnomes and all the many other names."

"I was an unwitting victim of that isolation," I said thoughtfully. "I wonder how many other people have a deep, submerged part of their psyche filled with such illuminating, yet inexplicable, experiences."

Once triggered, other memories of the difficulty of accepting metaphysical experiences came to the surface. The acceptance I now enjoyed had not been easily won. I remembered a time when Treenie, myself, and our children were living in a community and I had been confounded, when, picking some oranges one afternoon, a Being that identified with citrus spoke directly into my mind. I learned things that I previously had not known, but after the first rush of euphoria, the experience frightened me. During those years, the Intelligence of Nature spoke with me many times, teaching and soothing me, opening me to a reality of life that I could only glimpse in my most illumined moments. Many of those experiences were so metaphysical that I could not assimilate them into my daily life. There were heightened moments when I experienced such mystical beauty that I became oversensitized, and just living in the world became an ordeal of unbearable trauma. I had to learn to balance the visible with the invisible, the form with the formless; despite living in a community of forty people and despite having Treenie's invaluable support, I had never felt so isolated and alone in my life. There were times when I questioned my sanity. I struggled to accept my experiences as real, but they were so alien to my normal worldly reality that I tore myself apart as I struggled to adjust. I even tried sharing my experiences with community members and guests, hoping that if they accepted them, then maybe I could. But it did not work. On the contrary, the more other people accepted my metaphysical experiences, the more threatened I became.

This phase of my life was terminated rather abruptly. I was sharing a particularly sensitive experience with a group of community members one evening when a man I liked came in late, obviously tipsy. He had drunk enough wine to be offensive, and after listening to me for a while, he began to laugh. Before long, the whole group was laughing—just that—but from my perspective, they were laughing at *me*. I stopped talking and never again shared such things with more than one person in the community. When the group laughed, for me it felt like the ultimate rejection, yet it also served as the catalyst for the eventual development of my own self-acceptance.

From that evening, I realized that only by accepting my own reality could I find peace. I could not do this through any other person. Not even through Treenie. I had to learn to accept my own reality, even if it no longer fitted in with other people's. Eventually, following a series of uplifting mystical experiences that I documented in *Talking With Nature*, I came to accept that my world was expanding beyond all normal reality. My reverie ended abruptly as Thane spoke. "I have to leave now, but I never truly leave you. You are Thane; I am your purpose."

With those odd, challenging words, Thane walked away, his small figure vanishing rapidly.

"Wait," I called out, sprinting after him, but the huge hall was empty.

5

Dimensions of Reality

I close my eyes, and in the
closing stars wink out.
I dream of a long forgotten past,
of a future I once knew,
and in some other reality
I experience déjà vu.

"**D**amn," I muttered. "Everybody seems to vanish except me." Deciding to find my way out of the Temple of Learning, I wandered off in the direction where Thane had departed.

I rounded a tall, beautifully carved pillar. Intrigued, I ran my gaze up the pillar to the ceiling far above. Without any great surprise, I saw that the ceiling was not held up by the pillars but seemed to hover a shade above them, as though cushioned rather than supported. Gazing at the pillar, I noticed that the carvings depicted a deep canyon, slashed into ochre rocks among shimmering heat and cactus. The heat radiated out, enforcing the power of the carvings to a remarkable degree. As I stepped away, I stumbled over a few rocks, while the heat was so great I ducked under a wide, low tree into its shade.

It was happening again. Just when I least expected it,

another scene was claiming me. There was no temple. I crouched in the shade of a thick-leafed, thorny tree within the wide canyon, watching as an Indian made his way toward me. Abruptly, the impact of a powerful déjà vu nearly overwhelmed me. This had happened when I had recently been in America. Treenie and I were in Arizona, near Sedona, walking with a family toward one of the vortices of Earth power that we had been told about. As we walked, I felt irresistibly drawn to scramble up the rocks toward this very same tree. I had crouched there, watching this Indian approach. Now, past and present merged, and intuitively I knew that this experience would give birth to a potentially greater future. I knew this, yet I was held in the paradox of reviewing the past while aware of the present.

I watched the approach of the Indian in fascination. His movements were pure grace, like the ripple in a field of tall grass as the wind sends a supple wave along its crest. His feet seemed firmly planted on the earth, and metaphysically they were, but not a rock trembled or a grain of dust stirred at his passing. I stood slightly away from the tree as he reached me and felt again a strong shock of recognition. "White Bear!" I gasped.

Confusion wrapped me in silken threads, threatening to overwhelm the experience; then I shrugged it away. After all I had been through, surely I could handle this. While I allowed calmness to flow through me, I reviewed the powerful memories that had been triggered suddenly. I had once lived a long and fruitful physical life as White Bear. When I died, my spiritual progress and ability were such that I released my physical body through ceremony and remained as discarnate on Earth for another two hundred years of linear time. My nonphysical presence was known and respected among my people. When children were born, I was there, welcoming the newborn soul to its physical vehicle and sharing some of my wisdom. When the elderly died, I cleared their vision of delusions, showing those who were ready the truth of Self. I visited the sick, entering their psyches through their delirium, and with the easing of their fears, they returned to health. In the dreams of my people, I made myself known to them, weaving symbols to make clear their path in life.

I remembered all this in an instant. My confusion stemmed from trying to comprehend how I could meet another me face-to-face. My earlier experiences, which I recounted in *Journey Into Nature*, had involved me *becoming* that other me, never in me *confronting* me! Logic and reason, both excellent tools for a physical reality, were inadequate for dealing with this. So I accepted the greater reality, releasing my resistance and my need to understand.

White Bear nodded his approval. He knew exactly what had been going through my head; after all, we were One. Although we lived in different time-frame realities, we were aspects of the One Self. To meet face-to-face not only exposed the illusions of time, it also revealed the many levels of reality we are all involved in. Not accepting this makes no difference to its happening; it merely blinds us, making us captives of separation. We imprison ourselves.

"Welcome, Thane," he silently projected, laughing at my involuntary reaction.

"Don't be ridiculous. I'm not Thane." I expostulated. "But you are, Michael. If this were not so, it could not be my truth. Thane is the aspect of Self that is a disciple of truth. You have learned that becoming free is the birth of purpose, and your purpose is to share your truth." White Bear smiled warmly. "This is tricky, for truth means different things to different people. This is a paradox, for truth is only truth in timing, yet truth is always truth. Your purpose is to expand the awareness of those people who are open and receptive, working in the foreground of shaping reality. It is now very appropriate, for truth demands a harvest."

"I'm not too sure about that," I growled. "I've suffered and died for truth too many times. No more."

White Bear looked at me sternly. "Would you deny me my destiny? You have died, you say. Who, then, stands here before me? Are you an illusion? It was fear that died. We are unborn, undying. Your rejection of Thane has been epitomized in your reluctance. Yes, you have suffered in this ongoing role, suffered terribly, but can you show me one human Being who has not? Suffering has always been a human creation to reveal the lie of separation. Death was never the problem, for every death of a body reveals the truth of Self, yet the habit of separation reenacts itself over and over. For you, this is ended. It is timely now to release your Thane aspect of Self."

"Release Thane? What do you mean?"

Sitting cross-legged on the desert soil beneath the spreading tree, White Bear beckoned me to do likewise. While neither of us felt fatigue, the familiar ways of the body offered a comfort that is difficult to define.

"I mean that you are holding Thane restricted. He is a child within you, awaiting release. Thane—a disciple of truth! Your reluctance to accept this is a denial not only of your own truth but also of every aspect of Self that you are. Consider how blessed you are to have Treenie at your side. With Treenie, your truth is your togetherness. You are a soul-bonded pair. Together, you express a wisdom and innocence that is the essence of wholeness. When you live your reality, it is conveyed and imparted on levels of consciousness that far transcend the spoken word. This is a gift you share." White Bear gave me an enigmatic smile. "You are more than I, yet no more."

I realized now why Thane had appeared as a six-year-old. His age symbolized my reluctance to share our truth. But as for the last statement? I sighed. "If you know me as well as I know you, you'll know I detest riddles."

White Bear looked amused. "It's a riddle that will soon be solved; that I promise you."

I stared at him, in awe of our human complexity within the sheer simplicity of life. I needed to be simpler, more open to life. What I needed was not to need! No wants, no desires, no personal hang-ups! As I stared at White Bear, I noted that his metaphysical appearance continued to express the way he/I had looked when physical. His hair was literally snow white, yet his body looked no more than forty, lean and vital.

"Like me," he said, "you have no place that you can call home. To share your truth, you are a wanderer. Truth determines where you will manifest your energy, taking on an embodiment, and only truth will move you on. You cannot expect to live on your little mountain undisturbed. That is the attachment of your ego self. Set Thane free. There is no lasting comfort for you in places. Travel, inspire, help people wake up—and depart."

Reluctance surged. "Why are you saying my home isn't my home? I don't like that!"

"Michael." White Bear's word energy caressed me, soothing and caring. "I feel what you feel. I know. No *place* is home for you, neither must you claim it. You always become attached. Home for you can be no more than a resting place, a place to return to. However, you can love such a place, for love is not an attachment."

Although I felt petty, I resisted his words. I knew that I should be boundless, unconfined, and unrestricted, but all I could feel was reluctance!

"I happen to like where I live. I like being surrounded by the familiar. I like my family nearby, the trees, all the plants around me. I like growing bananas, pot plants, and tropical fish." I hesitated. "However, while I accept that these are my attachments, they belong to the Michael me. Tell me, why is my higher purpose in opposition to my personality? I'm a sensitive person. I dislike crowds, cities, and dogma. So what is required of me? I'll tell you. Spend time in crowds and cities, the breeding ground of dogma! Ugh!"

To my surprise, White Bear chuckled, an expression of admiration on his features. His chuckle became a full laugh, and he fell back, laughing uproariously. Nothing is more infectious than laughter, and soon I, too, was laughing in complete abandon, even more so because I knew we were laughing at me.

Strangely, the laughter seemed to resolve something. It was as though some long past dislocation had been relocated, but in a different place. Most odd. I was taken aback when I heard my next question, as though I had accepted something and forgotten to tell me about it! "Anyway, where am I supposed to travel?" I asked.

"Treenie will know. Unlike you, she follows her destiny of high knowledge with willingness and grace. However, it is time for me to release this frame. I, too, have finished my separate embodiments. I am White Bear only as a reference name. Just as you must release Thane by expressing him, so must you give expression to me."

In one swift move, White Bear was on his feet. Startled, I sprang to mine. He stepped forward to embrace me, and in doing so, he merged into me. Strangely, although I felt shocked, I had intuitively known that this is what he would do. Without question, I felt more whole, and, dare I say it, less reluctant!

I expected that this synthesis with a past time would end right there, but as I physically left the shade of the tree, the heat blasted me. I joined Treenie, Tom, and Linda, along with their children, and we trekked back to their huge Silverado. The air conditioner soon provided a respite from the heat. We were on our way back to Phoenix from a trip to the awesome Grand Canyon, and visiting the vortex had been a diversion. As Tom drove us toward Sedona, I was acutely aware that my physical personal self of that time had resisted all that White Bear had said. It was the metaphysical me of the present that had experienced the deep laughter and synthesis of Self. The reluctant me in America was all set to dismiss the incident as a heat-induced hallucination, when we drove past a small street on the outskirts of Sedona. Shock reverberated right through me.

"Tom," I squawked. "Would you mind backing up to that street we just passed."

A moment later, Tom had swung around and I reread the street sign: WHITE BEAR ST.

As the me in America accepted all that had happened, I was released from that time frame.

❋

I stood by the pillar in the Temple of Learning, with a most profound appreciation for all that the name implied. As I stared one last time at the carving, I noticed a change: The cacti in the desert were flowering!

I looked around for Thane or Seine, but I was alone. By now I knew exactly why I was in this temple, and I doubted that I would find an exit one moment before my reluctance was fully resolved. With no clear idea of where to go, I continued on the way I had begun earlier, walking past the pillar and around the corner.

I walked into an area of plants. Their beauty wrenched a gasp from me, for mixed and mingled were plants from many realities. How I knew, I was not sure; the feeling was one of recognition. Green was the only color, but there were shades and degrees of green that had yet to be expressed on planet Earth. Even the light had turned green, yet it was a green of health and vitality, of some ethereal chlorophyll and oxygen mixing in a blend of energy that could never quite happen in a physical reality.

"Maybe you limit the future of Earth," Seine suggested as he emerged from a cluster of ferns.

I gazed at him thoughtfully, unsurprised by his sudden appearance. "Yes. You could be right. I wouldn't want to do that. Perhaps this *is* the plant life of a future Earth. A possible future, anyway."

Seine smiled at me fondly, and again I noticed that, like a dolphin, his features seemed designed for smiling.

"You have experienced two aspects of Self," he said, "but another aspect remains. No, not an aspect of Self," he corrected, "but more of a fulcrum for the aspects you have now embraced. Thane holds your purpose; White Bear, your wisdom." His smile held amusement. "You hold your reluctance! Of course, there are many more aspects of Self—aspects in numerous dimensions and realities—but the aspects you are meeting are keys to the release of your purpose, your Thane Self."

I waited, saying nothing. I knew that there was more to come.

"Among these plants is an underground chamber. It connects with a number of chambers that are being built in your Earth reality, in particular with the one in which you meditated at Woodstock."

I remembered the incident very well. Treenie and I had visited the Wittenburg Center to give a weekend workshop. I had entered the chamber, intrigued, and spontaneously I sat down to meditate. From that moment, I had pushed everything that happened into my deep subconscious, away from memory.

"To forestall your suspicions, I want you to know that I am not attempting to trick you. I am asking you to enter the chamber in this room. You will return to the experience you so thoroughly rejected. Once in, there is no way out except by resolution. I can only say that your remaining reluctance is embedded in your inability to face a certain truth." Seine paused, a strange, inscrutable expression on his face. "You can of course refuse to enter the chamber."

I gave a strangled laugh, half angry, half genuinely amused. "Seine, you are one tricky Being. You are using openness and honesty to disarm me. Now I have nowhere to hide, no excuses."

He looked very smug.

Knowing that Seine had offered me a choice of no choice at all, I decided to get into it at once. Ignoring him and his smug, wide smile, I pushed my way into the dense vegetation ahead. The first puzzle was how all this abundance of plants could be growing directly out of the glowing floor. There was no sign of any rich, fertile soil. I had little time to ponder on it, however, for I quickly came to a clearing that revealed the chamber. The chamber appeared identical to the one I had entered before. White Bear and the chamber: these had been my two major confrontations in America. White Bear I could deal with; the chamber I had buried deep in my subconscious, along with all the other experiences that were too difficult.

A dome of excavated soil covered the underground chamber. Intuition suggested that this dome did not exist in the Temple of Learning at all. I had the feeling that the mural, the pillar, and now this domed chamber were all Doors into past or future realities. Participants would see whatever was appropriate to them, triggering their own involvement. I stood speculating on this for some moments, aware of my reluctance to enter. I had blanked out what had happened in the chamber previously, and I was not sure I cared to revitalize it. And that bit about no way out without resolution was not very enticing. With a grumble at cosmic teachers in general, I cautiously entered the underground chamber.

❊

The smell of soil was as strong as ever, and I was again attracted to the crystals in the center of the chamber. I had the feeling that this experience was somehow different from before, and I waited for a merging with the past reality to take place. Nothing happened. This was a metaphysical me in a reality Beyond. Too late, I realized that Seine had tricked me after all. No wonder he looked so smug. Squatting near the crystals, I tried to figure out where the entrance had gone. Now I knew that skulduggery was involved. With no way in or out, it was very different from last time. The chamber was lit by what I can only describe as an Earth light, dim but clear. I felt no fear, only a mild trepidation.

How and when the other Being appeared, I have no idea. All I knew was that I was no longer alone. The Being who regarded me from across the chamber was the reason I had previously blocked out the experience. It was a bit taller than I and insectlike. It stood upright on two legs not much thicker than sticks. It was lean, very lean—or narrow—whichever applies. It had what appeared to be folded wing cases on its back and a very small head. If brains are always carried in heads, then this creature had no brain, which was a puzzle, for a high intelligence literally emanated from this Being.

Its head, while diminutive compared to mine, was certainly in proportion to its skeletal body. Very small mandibles indicated a mouth, and its eyes were narrow, iridescent slits of obsidian black. Four sticklike arms completed the picture, yet they appeared so natural that two arms would have looked quite ridiculous. Intelligence was not the only thing that the Being emanated; benevolence also radiated out so strongly that I now found it impossible to feel alarm.

Nonplussed, I trotted out the usual trite questions: "Who are you? Where are you from?"

The reply was more strongly telepathic than anything I had yet encountered. Perhaps this was because there was nothing that remotely resembled a human mouth, or even a chance of externalizing speech. But the reply was very clear and precise.

"Identifying me is not important, but if it helps, I am from Ceti, a very distant planetary system."

I decided to be honest. "I have trouble with these planets other Beings come from. Suppose you come from a planet that our space probes indicate are incapable of supporting life. How does that add up?"

"It adds up to the limitation of your space probes. All

physical life on planet Earth is three-dimensional. This means that your space probes can only investigate three-dimensional realities. This may very well mean that on a three-dimensional level a planet is a fiery furnace or is sub-zero gas, but that is no indication of other dimensional realities."

The flow of words stopped, and I felt inquiry. "Fine, I guess I can accept that." I replied.

"I come from a six-dimensional reality," it continued. "Whereas you are now metaphysically here, I am here in a dimensional physicality of choice—"

"Now you've lost me," I intervened. Although this Being could not laugh—its externalized skeleton would not allow it—very clearly I felt and heard merriment!

"We are masters of the nonphysical," it continued. "We can travel anywhere and 'anywhen' at will. Whatever dimensional changes are required, we can make them. Density and form are not fixed for us, although we usually maintain our own natural appearance, as you see me now. On our home planet, however, we enjoy a physicality that bears no resemblance to any physicality of yours. Without belittling you, a mind held by three-dimensional reality could not even conceive of the physicality to which I refer."

"Hmmm." I was at a loss for words until along came another question. "So why are we both here?"

There was no reply, and feeling that I should approach the Being instead of keeping a distance between us, I slowly walked up to it. I had thought that its body casing was a blue so dark it merged into black, but close up, a different color was revealed. The body casing was a dark blue shot with amethyst, with an insubstantial but closely webbed fabric of luminous sky blue over the entire body, excluding legs and arms.

"Do you fly?" I asked, indicating the wing cases.

"These are not wings. The casing encloses apparatuses that are built in with my body suit."

I realized then that the body suit was the sky blue fabric. "May I touch?" I asked. There was no spoken confirmation, but I felt it. When I touched the fabric, it felt no more substantial than cobwebbing, yet a feeling of high tensile strength translated into my fingertips. With this Being, touch carried its own translation, so I touched its body. Instantly, I had an impression of endless space, yet space of infinite light, without a trace of darkness. And under my fingers I felt love! Any last anxieties were immediately banished. Maybe it was this that prompted an answer to my unanswered question.

"We are here for you. It is time for you to remove some deeply implanted inner blocks you have established. You have long held the knowledge of other Beings in your consciousness. This, together with your knowledge of various aspects of Self, has led to an inner confusion. You are now uncertain about the true nature of your own Being. Your reluctance is partly based on this confusion."

I gasped. It was as though the Being had reached into the deepest recess of my consciousness and plucked out my subconscious, hidden fear, revealing it with astonishing detail and clarity.

"How did you know all that?"

"I know, for I am a Coordinator."

"Er . . . what do you coordinate?"

The Being faced me squarely, and it no longer seemed odd or bizarre. "We coordinate the movement and expansion of sentient awareness. Humanity is part of that movement. However, you are the reason I am here right now. You are my concern."

The Being emanated compassion. It held out a "hand" feathered with flexible appendages like wire, all having the ability to flex and move in any direction. If fingers give us a manipulative ability, this "hand" was a hundred times more efficient. I took it without hesitation, holding tightly, but there was no need. In that instant, we were elsewhere.

❊

We stood in a crystal valley I recognized. The memory had been revived and revisited earlier as I described in *Journey Into Nature,* and it had ended in mystery. I had been able to accept the previous experience, but it had left me feeling unfulfilled. Now, I again stood in the valley, surrounded by mountains of crystal, towering ten or maybe fifteen thousand feet into the alien sky. Milky at the base, the color gradually leached out, until the uppermost reaches were transparent spires of crystal clarity.

"This is where I . . . " My words faded out. It knew. I didn't doubt that it knew more about me than I did. I felt very disadvantaged. I didn't even know its name. "What's your name?" I asked abruptly.

"No names, please. In truth, I am nameless, as are all

of my kind. We express an imprint of Being that identifies us, yet does not separate in the manner of a name. The emanation you feel from me is as close to a name as I have or need."

I now felt a more complex emanation. It contained the earlier impression of high intelligence, mixed and mingled with a feeling of space and purpose. Very odd.

"Your summary is surprisingly accurate. While you missed all the subtleties, you got the essence. Please, you are at ease with my presence; allow my namelessness to open you to a deeper connection in consciousness. Know me as an inner response, not an outer label. Connect, for this is your destiny. In the connection is direct knowing."

Within the valley, I watched the Being I knew to be another aspect of Self complete the experiment of psyche transference. The previous time I had become One with the Being and experienced the experiment, but it had left me devoid of any knowledge about it or about that aspect of Self.

Once again, I saw the immense alien sun rise above the crystal mountains in a single smooth movement. Light, more powerful than I can describe, bounced from spire to spire, gaining and building in power. Finally, it caught the largest spire and, following a known and calculated trajectory, it hit the tall, thin humanoid figure in the center of the valley. Again, even though I stood apart this time, the shock blasted me into a blankness, and my psyche reached out across all eternity. Instantly, I *knew*. I connected with all the other aspects of my Self, and I knew. During what seemed forever-in-a-second, Self reached out into the infinite Beyond, and I also experienced the Beings that my mind had fostered in fear. The Being who had conducted the experiment in psyche transference held the key. He was old in our terms, many thousands of our years old, and his knowledge was so prodigious that I could not even conceive of most of it, let alone store it. That Being had willingly paid a terrible price, for his physical body was literally atomized, but he consciously became One with all aspects of Self. His experiment had been a triumph.

In that timeless, forever second, I reexperienced many of the aspects of Self. I was the slender Blue Being that had so disturbed me when, years ago, I had dreamt about it. In the dream I was about five feet tall, graceful and elegant. I had abilities unknown to humanity, and I knew who I was and where I came from. Suddenly, in the dream, a voice intercepted. "He is not ready for this. It is far too early." Then the dream ended, and I woke up. On waking, I remembered the name and place and other details, but as I reached for a pen and pad to write them down, I felt my mind deliberately fuzzing. That was it. I remembered the incident, but none of the details. I was so distressed I buried it in the subconscious murk along with my other inexplicable experiences.

Now, I was in their city of living glass that was shaped and formed in full cooperation into swirling whirlpools of multicolored buildings. Transparent tinted bubbles hung on threads of spun glass, rather like dewdrops on a strand of spider's web. Everywhere, color blossomed and bounced in subtle shades of ever-changing rainbow hues, and the familiarity and beauty were so great that I wept. The Blue Beings bathed me in thoughts of love. Some I knew and recognized, and within the love that revitalized me, I felt the unspoken promise of a return. Even now, I neither knew who they were or where they lived, but I was content.

As all this gently faded, into my awareness came my Self as the golden woman of my future. She also I had recently experienced. Well over six feet tall, she had the classic appearance of a mythical goddess, with an intelligence and intellect to match. We were in a city where cultural and social requirements met in a blend of architecture and Nature of breathtaking design. Gold was the predominant color of all building materials, and, as in the Temple of Learning, the buildings were a composite of material and thought, brought together into a creative manifestation of cathedral beauty. Together—as One—we walked along a moving strip of light laid casually on a bed of smooth pebbles. We entered a building, one suspiciously like the Temple of Learning, and joined a large number of other people. I recognized one Being as an aspect of Treenie, but my attention was held by the immense aura of a radiant golden Being standing on a pedestal where all could see him.

He spoke with a quiet penetration, and all heard him telepathically. He affirmed that we were all volunteers—and I realized that there were thousands of us in this building that could adapt to any numbers—and that the time had come for us to honor our commitment. We were to travel back in time to a time before this. We would have to incarnate into our own past, taking on once more the trauma that accompanied such action. We would be fitting into the time slot that most befitted and compelled us, yet within us all, the seed of our greater knowing would remain. Diminished, it was up to us to rekindle that knowing, for only in this way would we find the passion and commitment to encompass and express our purpose. The outcome of all this hinged on Earth change as new vibrational pulses swept the galaxy during a time of Earth flux. I realized that our present-time Earth is facing these howling gales of change—right now!

Other aspects of Self became known to me, one after another, and my earlier confusion was resolved. Previously, the puzzle of nonterrestrial Beings as aspects of Self had remained unanswered. Now, I had expanded in my experience of Self, which compelled me to face a truth that applied to each and every human Being. I accepted that I, as Self, lived in an Earth-time reality, while I also lived as other aspects of Self in other dimensions, all expressing Self in the infinite Beingness of Now. All this I could accept easily because it remained unthreatening. The truth that was so difficult was the one that had given birth to my reluctance, a deeply hidden, unapproachable truth— until now! In all those many aspects of Self, one aspect had chosen to express the unity of the Whole: me!

With this realization, I quailed. Now I knew what White Bear had meant when he told me I was more than he, yet no more. I also realized that denying any aspect of Self meant that, to a degree, I denied all aspects of Self. Self is inseparable. With the birth of this new insight, I hardly noticed that the insectlike Being had taken my hand and that we were back in the chamber in the Temple of Learning.

"Why me?" I whispered. "I'm too simple for such as this. I accept that I made the choice, but that was a greater I in a different time/reality. Why isn't one of those other aspects of Self, with their vastly superior knowledge and capacities, the one to unify the Whole Self?"

Benevolence, compassion, caring, and love all emanated from the Being. "Of all the many aspects of Self, you have the greatest capacity to embrace the Whole. It demonstrates the power of *simplicity!*"

Then the Being did a strange thing. It stepped close to me, and taking my hands, it put my palms on the top of its small head. A silent explosion of pink light went off in my skull. For a moment I reeled; then the impact of powerful sensory perception overwhelmed the dizziness. I perceived a great respect from this Being. With a shock, I knew that this Being felt privileged to coordinate my framework of reference to Self. There was a feeling of "Mission accomplished!" I experienced an empathy as I embraced many of the hitherto unreachable emanations. For the first time with this Being, I radiated love in return for the love I received.

"What do I do with what I know, with what I am?"

The emanations of care and love were more powerful than ever. "You live, you love, you share, you give. With Treenie, you focus on the awakening of the people of Earth. Life will continue to open you and teach you, and Self of many aspects and levels will express through you. Together, as a soul-bonded pair, you are agents of change, moving in and out of people's lives. Together, you promote the alchemy of change. And as you are, so, too, are thousands of others. You are neither more nor less important than any of these. You are life unfolding life, love expressing love. Just as this is your truth, so, too, it is the truth of every human Being."

I felt the love emanating from the Being, but as I took my hand from the top of its head, I was alone in the chamber.

※

Although the entrance was now clearly visible, I stood alone for a long while before I walked back out. This experience had differed in very many ways from the previous time. Although it initially followed the same basic format, everything was greatly extended and expanded, particularly my relationship with the insectlike Being. My earlier difficulty had obviously limited and restricted the whole experience. Before, I had blocked and rejected; now, I had encompassed and accepted.

I realized also that I was no longer reluctant to express my purpose! This was a good feeling.

Seine was waiting, his luminous moonlight eyes fixed on mine. He said nothing, but the expression on his face conveyed more than words ever could. He turned, and in his inexplicable way, he vanished within taking three paces. I slowly made my way from the area of plants and found an open doorway facing me. Knowing that it was time to leave the Temple of Learning, I hurried toward it. As I stepped through the Door, time spun and twisted.

❋

I opened my physical eyes. I was at home, sitting in my comfortable chair. Apart from the usual heavy and sluggish feeling that always accompanied being back in a physical body once more, I felt fantastic.

6

The Illusion of Time

*Spherical time is an eternal moment
in an infinite reality.
Linear time simply gives us access
to infinity in acceptable measures.
We learn and grow through cause and effect,
the great gift of linear time.*

I sat for quite a while in silent contemplation. All that had happened remained clear and fresh in my mind. Was my reluctance finally laid to rest? Earlier, as each aspect of Self had revealed a facet of my reluctance, I had thought that facet to be the whole problem. I should have known better! Much earlier experiences had shown that I had ended several lives under torture for being a heretic, and that the trauma had amassed an enormous reluctance to ever repeat such pain and fear again. I had learned, however, that the more we seek to avoid something unpleasant, the more strongly we attract it. Yet as I persistently whittled away at it, the shape and character of my reluctance had changed, baffling me. The insectlike Being had finally helped me resolve my reluctance, drawing the deep subconscious rejection of responsibility from the depths of my psyche.

The sound of a voice attracted me, and I wandered into the kitchen. Treenie was on the phone, chuckling at something she was being told. She smiled at me.

"Hello, my darling," she said quietly, her hand over the mouthpiece.

While she finished her conversation, I put the kettle on. The only way to a good cup of tea is definitely physical!

After talking for a few more minutes, Treenie hung up the phone. "That was a person in Washington State who wants to organize talks and seminars for us over there."

"So when do we go?"

Treenie raised her eyebrows in surprise.

"Isn't this where you begin to squirm?" she asked. "Normally you start the 'I'm too busy' routine or 'Do we have to?' or 'Maybe another year.' To what or to whom do we owe this change? Or is this some subtle joke?"

"Would I joke about something like this?" I asked with mock indignation.

It took me quite a while to share all that had happened. I had trouble in relating the time scales involved—or, should I say, the lack of linear time—as I talked about the events that had unfolded in that rich and detailed metaphysical reality.

"I don't know why, but I was surprised that you also know Seine," I said.

Treenie looked thoughtful. "This is where we are very different, you and I. You have had this wonderful experience, and you retain the memory and knowing of it. You have access to a metaphysical reality that seems as available to you as walking from one room into another.

"I don't experience it like that. When I sleep, I am aware of two levels. One is a normal dream state; the other is far deeper, a place of power and reality, where I am more awake than I can ever be in a physical state. I meet people and Beings in this place. I know this. I teach, and I am taught. Time has no meaning at all, and on inner levels, I am nourished and replenished. However, when I wake up in the morning, I have no clear memory of it, just a deep intuitive knowing."

She frowned in concentration. "I don't find this as easy to put into words as you, but I know I know Seine, even though I don't remember him. Does that make sense?"

I nodded vigorously. "It makes perfect sense. I guess the incident with the Roman soldiers happened in the same way. Or do you remember it?"

Treenie shook her head, her eyes and face shaded from the light streaming in the glass doors. "No, I don't. What I find remarkable is the time factor in all this. I realize that in a greater reality time is *not* a factor, but it is so much a part of our everyday lives that it cannot be ignored."

"What do you mean?" I asked.

"Well, the experiences you just shared with me sound as though they took a long time, yet—" She put up her hand to forestall my interruption. "Let me finish. Yet I know that time was not involved. However, you were in that reality no more than forty-five of our minutes, but you had what seems like ages of experience in more than one time frame. I haven't been asleep during that linear time, yet I was involved. Obviously, my involvement happened at some other time in my sleep, yet you were able to access that time and it became a present moment in a greater reality." She paused. "Would you agree with all that?"

"Yes. I think you summed it up brilliantly. The only thing

I would add is that all of time and all realities occupy the same moment—an eternal Now. We need linear time, for in our human development we are not yet ready to access infinity, even though we are infinite Beings. We learn and grow through cause and effect, the great gift of linear time."

Our discussion continued for a while, but Treenie had mail to answer and things she wanted to do.

I watched her a few minutes later as she sat at her desk, absorbed in the tasks she so enjoyed. I reflected once again on how fortunate I am to be married to Treenie. To live in a partnership of such in-depth compatibility is a rich blessing. I thought about White Bear's reference to us as a soul-bonded pair. That Treenie and I were a soul-bonded pair I did not doubt, but what exactly did this mean?

"What is a soul-bonded pair?" I called out.

Treenie gave me a strange look. "Apart from the obvious, it's something you are going to learn about quite soon."

"Oh. How do you know that?"

Again, she gave me that odd look. "I don't really *know* it. I *feel* it."

I shrugged. I could wait. One thing I had learned about was the timing of knowing. Intellectual knowledge can be gained at any time, but actualized knowing only happens in perfect timing. And we are the timing!

✳

A few weeks later, in the grip of a drought, a very welcome and heavy downpour of rain had freshened up the light forest scrub that surrounded our house. A steep gully nearby was generally dry, and I wanted to see if there had been enough rain for seeping water to be flowing. I had noticed that a few fan palms grew there, along with creeping ferns and bracken, but I had yet to see even a trickle of water.

I scrambled down into the depths of the gully, and I was pleased to see a thin gleam of water as it flowed over the shelves of slaty rock. Fresh water attracts me. So much life abounds along the water's edge. Here there was scarcely an inch deep of sluggish water, yet it attracted some large red dragonflies and their more dainty cousins, the damselflies.

I followed the gully, carefully turning over rocks where the trickle flowed, then putting them back in their original positions. Occasionally, I spied small frogs, mostly brown and inconspicuous. As my eyes became adapted to the observation mode, more and more wildlife became obvious. Soon, I was totally absorbed, watching, seeing, being with. When the loud scuffle of an echidna partly under a nearby log broke the deep silence, I was momentarily startled.

I walked over to the strange creature. Commonly known as spiny anteaters, which nicely describes them, echidnas are one of only two kinds of animals in the world that both lay eggs and suckle their young. Dinosaurs used to do that. I watched the echidna for a while as it clawed its way into a small nest of white ants under the log. A nearby friendly tree offered good back support, so I sat down, leaning against it contentedly. Just fancy, I thought, this echidna has no idea that I am sitting close by. I don't even fit into its framework of reference. Here I am, with the ability to hold its future in my hands, to interfere with it or leave it alone, and it knows nothing of this. It is totally preoccupied with getting its food. Everything is basic and immediate. I sat back, relaxed and comfortable in the warm shade. The shadows seemed to shift and blur.

❋

I released my focus on the physical world, and I was hardly surprised when a silent voice came into my awareness.

"How different is humanity?"

While my physicality never quite vanished to my awake physical senses, the metaphysical reality that emerged had my full attention.

I stood with Seine on a farm. It was an arable farm, and as I stared, I realized that it was my father's farm in England. A much younger me was sitting in a hedgerow, a .22 rifle in my lap. Out of sheer curiosity, I walked close to him, and called out, "Michael."

My words were silent, and he heard nothing. Seine and I stood by his side, yet that youthful me had no idea that we were there.

"You are right. That younger me is as unaware of us as the echidna was of me."

"Is."

"What do you mean?"

"Is unaware of you, not was. That reality is still happening. Physically, you are still close to the echidna. You must

111

encompass the dimensions of time and reality as all happening *Now*."

I understood what Seine was saying, but I was a bit disgruntled at this very unaware me of my youth.

"How often does this happen?" I asked. "How often is something that happens in the past or present involved with a different reality of another time frame?" I laughed. "I'm not even sure I know how to ask the question without getting muddled."

"It happens very often with all people, but they are rarely aware of it as you now are."

"Am I able to influence this younger me in any way?"

"Here is your opportunity to find out."

We watched as Michael steadied the rifle, aiming at a hare as it loped across the field a few hundred yards away.

"Don't shoot," I silently projected, as powerfully as I could. "Experience the hare." Young Michael held the aim steady, and I despaired. How well I knew my old skill with a rifle. But then I remembered the incident.

"He won't shoot," I said to Seine. "I remember now. But I still don't know if this is a result of my influence."

"Just observe, and feel."

The hare jigged its way across the field in a series of sudden and eccentric bounds, quite obviously having fun. It stopped suddenly, then, turning at right angles to its previous direction, it headed straight for Michael.

He sat still as a statue, and I knew he was spellbound by the wonder of it. From two to three hundred yards' distance, the hare was quickly no more than five yards away and still coming. Only inches away from Michael's feet, it stopped so abruptly that its hind legs bounced into the air. Michael and the hare were staring eye to eye, the gun forgotten.

That younger me held his breath, frightened to make any sound that might break the magic of the moment. Then, as though it had all the time in the world—and it had—the hare turned around and loped away.

Young Michael's breath was exhaled in a gush. The rifle came easily to his shoulder as he followed its progress through the telescopic sights, but his finger never went near the trigger.

"My God! Nobody will ever believe this," he said aloud.

"I believe it," I told him, but he was as blind and deaf to me as that echidna.

❈

Seine casually touched my shoulder, and instantly we were somewhere else—in a small country town. It felt odd to be walking down the middle of the high street, knowing that nothing physical could see or touch us.

"I did influence me. I know it."

Seine smiled, but he made no further reference to the incident. "Look around you. Observe everything you can see."

"Everything?"

"Just observe. You will understand."

I will never know whether an adjustment was made to my metaphysical perception, or if his power of suggestion increased my own developing ability. All I know is that the street now held far more than everyday people. I gazed around. There was now a mixture of physical and metaphysical people on the streets, and there were Beings that were clearly nonhuman.

"Is this a normal scene on many levels of reality, or is it exaggerated for my benefit?" I gasped.

"Quite normal, Michael. As you correctly surmised, this is normality on many dimensional levels. In fact, there is considerably more, for much is beyond your perception."

I stared around me. As I watched, I became aware that although there seemed to be many Beings involved, there was no crowd, at least not in any one reality. There was no more than a scattering of the regular townspeople, and each metaphysical reality seemed to be in perfect juxtaposition with all the others. All somehow occupied the same space, but in very different dimensions or zones. Throughout all this, a few otherworldly Beings moved with unhurried grace.

"Good heavens, look. There is a Being like you," I said, turning to Seine. Even as I indicated, they were facing each other in seeming silence, each radiating their beautiful natural smiles. I knew that they were in deep telepathic communication. I also realized that by sharing spheres of knowing, they could communicate more effectively in moments than a couple of humans could in weeks.

With Seine occupied, I decided, out of curiosity, to follow one of the people. I chose an elderly woman, wrapped in a shawl against the cool wind that funneled down the street. She had a slight limp, and she was carrying a full and heavy shopping basket that dragged at her right arm. I felt a deep despair within her. Every now and then she coughed, a deep phlegmy sound that tore at her throat. I had the sudden realization that this could well be her last dreary walk down the high street. I wanted to help her, but as far as she was concerned, I was not there. I could do nothing.

We reached a small thatched cottage, its door literally opening onto the pavement. I followed the old woman indoors, and I came to another dimension of being, for there in the room, a young man was waiting. I could easily see him, but she could not. Equally, he could not see me.

I could also hear him. "Grandma, I've come to help you over to the other side." She, however, heard nothing. I stared at him aghast. What nonsense was this? There *is* no other side. All the many dimensions of being are held in a multidimensional Now. This includes so-called death. Being dead does not mean we change sides as if in some cosmic cricket match; it's a transition in reality. Having made the transition, surely he knew this?

I walked over to him and, on impulse, placed my hand on his head. Instantly, I knew his reality. As easily as that, I had an insight into his consciousness. He did not know truth. Death held no answers; it merely held a continuity of his previous beliefs. He believed that in dying he had crossed over to the other side. The other side of what, exactly, he had no idea, but it was a belief he was not yet ready to relinquish. However, his intent toward his grandmother was kind and caring.

Curious, I placed my hand briefly on her brow. And again I had the clear insight of another person's reality. She shivered, dragging her hat off her head. "Someone walked over my grave," she muttered to herself, quite unaware of her company.

For a brief moment, the young grandson frowned and stared in my direction. As I watched his eyes, I wondered if he might see me, but he lost focus almost immediately. His restrictive beliefs and limits were too powerful.

"Don't you worry yourself, Grandma. I'll wait for you. You'll be ready to cross over tonight."

Realizing that I could add nothing of value to the situation, I walked out through the wall and into the street. To my surprise, a Being that was the pure essence of beauty was waiting for me. There was no defined shape to this Being, no form to which I could relate; rather, it expressed itself as the *feeling* of beauty. I intuitively knew that it would appear to any other Being in whatever way related to that Being's perception of beauty. For me, I experienced a feeling of waterfalls and unicorns, mixed and merged with the feeling of beautiful music. Beyond that, I am unable to describe it.

This Being did not speak to me, but I felt the power of suggestion moving into me. No words, just feeling. The suggestion seemed to be that I step closer into its energy.

I did so. To be honest, I was almost overwhelmed by the beauty. Something so pristine pure, without humor, passion, or words, was slightly unnerving.

※

As I entered the energy field of this Being of Beauty, the whole town went through a gradual transformation.

116

The town melted away as the dominant feature, and a landscape of multicolored snow and ice was revealed. Immediately, I realized I was mistaken. I had tried to give a name to the nebulous forms and shapes around me, but I was wrong. In the vague appearance of snow and ice, I saw living plasma of unworldly color engaged in what appeared to be a slow and precise dance. As I watched, I was enfolded in the dance—a dance that was the expression of Intelligent Beauty.

Just as the Being was Beauty, so also beauty described this reality. It was not, nor would it ever be, vaguely human. Yet it occupied the same space as the small country town. Silently, I inquired what dimension this was, but any reply was meaningless. For a moment, I wondered why I was here, but then I knew. In some inexplicable way, just the experience of being here opened my perception to the unknown. I knew, without knowing how I knew, that each Being that visited this reality would perceive its surroundings in a different way. I realized that it is our mind that creates the world we live in, and consensus is an important part of that reality. Here, I had to trust my own experience of reality, knowing it was valid. The energy of Beauty released me, and, in a slow fade, . . .

※

. . . like watching a slide in a slow-shift projector, the town gradually reformed around me.

"That was a privilege," Seine said.

I could not speak. For long moments, tears blinded my

eyes, and I was so aware of the emotion in my physical body leaning against the tree in the gully that I felt I would be drawn back to it.

Seine placed a supple, strong, and densely furred hand on mine. The golden fur that covered his entire body was only fractional in length and, like a mole, was smooth in any direction. I felt the strength and reassurance. My emotions subsided, and I was able to remain in the metaphysical state.

"It was the beauty, Seine," I whispered. "I never dreamt that beauty could be a living expression. I don't understand it, because I know that's not possible, but it has done something to me—something inside my psyche."

I watched as discarnate humans mixed with incarnate people. The incarnate were normal and physical, while the discarnate humans were without physical bodies. Some were clearly bewildered, as though they did not yet know they were nonphysical, while a few walked among them with a clear purpose. I saw one lady glowing with light. She had the appearance one would ascribe to the classic angel.

"Who is she?" I asked Seine.

"Just watch."

She noticed us watching and walked over, clearly aware and comfortable with our presence.

"Hello, Seine."

"The stars smile on you," he replied in a formal way.

She laughed in delight. "You never forget, do you?"

They both chuckled at some private joke that obviously lay in their past—or future!

Seine turned, politely indicating me. "You, of course, know Michael, but I'm afraid he does not know that he knows you," he said, smiling disarmingly.

"Michael, this is the Lady Gold."

I was disconcerted to learn that I knew her, yet my memory refused to cooperate. And her name, the Lady Gold, was odd.

They spoke in silence, and I realized that spheres of information and experience were passing between them. One must have been tossed my way, for suddenly I knew that the Lady Gold supervised the teams of awake and aware discarnate humans that assisted the still sleeping, unaware souls who had recently died. As I learned this, I realized that in some cases, a few hundred years was still recent.

"It all depends on the rigid structures of their lives and the strength of their belief systems," the Lady Gold told me.

"Many of the open and flexible souls go straight into a reality change with obvious ease and delight. This is not so much determined by what they know, but by their openness and lack of fear. Generally speaking, beliefs about life are related to fear."

"What shocks me is the depths, levels, and intensity of all this," I said. "This is only a small country town. What ever must it be like in a city?"

"More confusion, more suffering, and much more intensity," she replied. "Light workers on many levels are forever weaving truth into the hearts of the incarnate and discarnate alike where receptivity will allow it, but my work is with those who are lost in their deaths."

She moved away as though she were a breath of fresh and golden mist on the lightest breeze.

＊

Seine put a hand on my shoulder, and once again everything changed. We stood in a hospital, but it was no earthly hospital.

A softly glowing light illuminated the whole area. Although I knew this was a hospital, it appeared as a merging and mixing of a building of great spiritual qualities with a valley of stunning natural beauty.

"I never knew that the role of beauty is so paramount to our wholeness," I whispered reverently as I gazed around. I perceived that there was an input from many levels of awareness and being in this hospital, but shining through it all was a beauty that was palpable—a beauty that was so luminous in its expression that the hospital was illuminated by its presence.

Seine looked pleased. "That is both perceptive and accurate. The patients in this hospital are generally human; all are nonphysical, but many of them are still alive in a physical reality."

"Oh! How are they here then?"

He beckoned me to accompany him, and we walked into the vast and extraordinary combination of garden/building. The tinkling of water as it fell over some rocks attracted us, and soon we were standing by a small waterfall. It was very different from normal physicality. It seemed that different rules applied here—if any did—for while some water fell, another column of water flowed upward to meet it. The meeting point of these two streams of water produced a mellow tinkling sound of ethereal beauty, as though angels and fairies were combining all their grace and skill to make the sound of life's continuity.

It was wholeness as a sound, a vibration of incredible healing. I listened, spellbound, as an inner wave of fresh energy flowed through me. I was so immersed in the waterfall that it took Seine several moments to draw my attention to other people in the immediate vicinity.

"Observe," he said silently. "And empathize. The people who come here are suffering from acute isolation, from the ravages of fragmentation, guilt, and despair."

For a moment, I thought Seine was joking, but as I felt an empathetic link with the despair of a young woman nearby, I knew better.

Realizing that I was invisible to her, I placed my hand briefly on her brow. Instantly, a picture formed in my inner vision, a motion picture involving the young woman. The picture was of a very recent scene from her life, but with the scene came a knowing of what had led up to it. Eva, for that was her name, a young, slim, brown-haired woman, had been having an extramarital affair. Her husband, Ken, had recently found out, and in his humiliation and anger, he had thrown her out of their home. Swearing that she would never see their two small children again, he had even thrown her clothes and personal items out of the house, then barred and bolted it against her.

In despair, she had driven her car to Lennie's—the other man—pouring out the whole story to him. To her utter astonishment, he rejected her. "You were okay for a bit of fun on the side," he said casually, "but that's all it ever was for me. I thought you felt the same way. It was just a brief fling."

"But . . . I thought you loved me," Eva whispered huskily.

Lennie looked surprised. "Love! You must be joking!" He glanced at his wristwatch. "Anyway, you'd better go. My wife will be home soon. She doesn't know anything about you, and I don't intend for her to find out."

He led Eva to the door, opened it, and pushed her out.

"It's all over, Eva, so get lost," he said with callous indifference.

She drove away in a daze, not knowing where to go. The fragments of her life lay in shattered pieces around her, and she felt more isolated and alone than she had ever known.

Eva drove past her home three times, her head in a whirl, as she once again reached the intersection at the end of her familiar road. She saw nothing of the truck that hit her as she drove unseeing into its path, and for six hours she hovered between life and death in the intensive care ward at the local hospital. The operations she underwent were successful, and Ken was notified.

Ken sat with her now, holding her hand, his face wet with tears. "It's okay," he murmured over and over. "It's all okay. I forgive you. I love you," he repeated in a monotone of misery, as he gazed at her slack and shockingly pale face.

I stared at Eva. Although her physical body lay in a hospital bed, this metaphysical Eva was sitting near the waterfall, clearly under its influence, yet dazed and unaware. I realized then that it was not her considerable injuries that pushed her toward death, but the despair in her psyche. She could not live with the sudden and devastating fragmentation of her life, the guilt and despair of her own deceit and foolishness.

"Can I help in any way?" I asked Seine.

"Do you remember the slum family that Thane revealed for you? You were able to help them."

"Yes! Of course. Love. If I love her for who she is, maybe she can find that ability for herself."

As my insight clarified, Eva's plight became clearer. Ken was a man of suppressed emotions, raised by parents of great emotional restraint. Eva craved affection, and in her search for a more demonstrative expression of love, she had fallen into the old, well-worn pitfall of sex. Now, her self-loathing held her physical recovery in abeyance.

Moving closer to Eva, I put my arms around her and gently held her. She was unaware of this either physically or metaphysically. I thought about the plight of humanity, seeing us as a multitude of caterpillars, unaware of our butterfly beauty and potential. She became the focus of my compassion for humanity, not in a personal way, but as an individual. I visualized her as the Being of Light she really is—as we all really are—and I held her lovingly.

It seemed only moments before she stirred from her lethargy, her eyes becoming clear and focused. It now became apparent that she could hear the sound of the waterfall, and I stood back from her.

"That's beautiful, just beautiful," she murmured to herself, and the beauty registered in her features as her face lit up with a new self-appreciation. She looked around, wide-eyed, yet it was clear that she felt only comfort and great inner nourishment in this strange hospital.

My vision took me back into the physical hospital where her body was stirring. How different. The auras of many of the nursing staff clearly indicated their dedication and care for their patients, but there was a brittle inflexibility in the atmosphere that sadly matched the hospital's sterility.

Although Eva lay in a screened-off section, this time I could see other, nonphysical Beings standing by some of the beds as the life of that particular patient hung in the balance.

It had never before occurred to me that hospitals in other dimensions catered to the very ill—hospitals that sought to cure the discord of the soul, rather than the injuries of the body. These ethereal hospitals worked in a synchronization unrealized by their physical counterparts, yet while the metaphysical hospital worked with the whole person for holistic healing, both were devoted to the care of human life. The real difference was vision. For the physical hospital, death was the end and was often considered a failure; for the other hospital, death was a transition, signaling the beginning of a new phase of growth and progress.

As I stood near Ken, my awareness encompassing the many levels of being that were involved, Eva's eyes flickered and opened.

"I'm so sorry, my darling," Ken said brokenly.

Eva's eyes widened. "You called me darling. You've never done that before. Don't stop."

"Darling . . . darling . . . darling," Ken said tearfully. "I didn't know how to say it. I promise you I'll never stop calling you darling—my darling."

I was back in the ethereal beauty of the metaphysical hospital. Eva was now an insubstantial shadow, gradually fading away as her focus in life was once more centered in a physical reality.

I had one last look at the reunited couple.

"I had an incredible dream," Eva was whispering sleepily. "I was held in the arms of an angel, and the most incredible music I have ever heard was washing over us. I think I was dying. Then there was love . . . and . . . "

She was alseep.

Back in the metaphysical realm, I looked at Seine in astonishment. "What did she mean? I was hugging her, not an angel."

He laughed. "Do you have any idea what a Light Being, human or otherwise, would look like in a normal person's reality? Anyway, that was the way her mind rationalized it."

I wondered how often we are one another's angels in the critical moments of severe pain, illness, and dying. Unsuspected, we each integrate into the lives of those we love—and the lives of others—on a level we could not mentally comprehend or accept. The bond of One humanity is more subtle than is physically apparent.

Seine and I walked slowly from the waterfall area, allowing ourselves to be drawn to wherever felt appropriate.

"That really was not a difficult case," I said. "Eva seemed to recover very quickly."

"Two points for you to consider. First, we are in spherical time, so you cannot measure the linear time-frame reality. Two, the time from her accident to the time of her recovery in physical terms has no relation to the time she spent in this hospital. However, I acknowledge that the love she felt from you, as you held her, did much to assist her recovery. As you learned in the slum, it is humanity that must uplift humanity, caring for one another and for Self. You shared the gift of Self-love with her."

Remembering what Seine had said about some of the patients still being physically alive, the obvious hit me.

"Are some of the patients here physically dead?"

"Yes, many are."

"How does an unaware person deal with the fact that, for a while, this is a one-way ticket?"

"Suppose you find out for yourself."

Seine's hand touched me lightly, and . . .

※

. . . with no warning I was in a light aircraft. I felt as though I were physical, for I had my own seat, and the engine noise and vibration were as large as life. When I pinched myself, I was shocked that I could feel it. Despite this, I felt a degree of calm clarity and perception that transcended my normal physical reality. However, when the engine suddenly faltered, spluttering, the alarm I felt was 100 percent genuine.

I was relieved that Treenie was not with me. Where I was going alone was a complete mystery, and why, but all those considerations became superficial as the engine cut out. I heard the pilot's voice over the intercom, but his words were drowned by the pounding of my own heart. Although the feeling that this was not quite real hovered in my awareness, there was no way out. With all the energy I could muster, I wished myself back to Seine, but I remained strapped in the seat of a plane that was falling out of the sky.

When, following a muffled explosion, a large piece of metal tore away from the front of the aircraft to dance across the outside of my window, I blanched at what awaited.

People screamed, and I smelled the offensive stink of fresh vomit. With the other passengers, I followed the well-established drill of getting my head down. The scream of a dying aircraft drowned all other sound as it hurtled toward the earth, tearing at my eardrums.

This is it! Nobody would survive. For a brief moment I played with my grim joke—no bodies! This was an obvious certainty. One moment the scream of tortured metal filled all dimensions of space and sound; then came the most profound and absolute silence.

I had no awareness of a crash or the impact. Was I dead? Was I still with the plane? I lifted my head from between my knees and cautiously looked around.

"Wow! When you playact, you certainly go for real. Are you all right, my darling?" Treenie was standing by my side, looking a little anxious.

We were surrounded by the wreckage of the aircraft, scattered in shreds of ruin over quite a wide area. Miraculously, there was no fire, not even the smell of aviation fuel. Only in that moment did I realize that I had never been physically in the plane, yet the illusion had been strong enough for me to believe in it.

I felt shaken and vaguely nauseated. The silence was overwhelming after the scream of the plunging aircraft. We were in a lightly wooded area; a broken tree had impaled the fuselage of the plane as efficiently as I used to spear a rat. Each crumpled wing was flattened to the ground some distance away on either side, as though hugging the soil in a grotesque parody of thanksgiving.

"I think so," I croaked as I clung to her. "How did you get here?"

"This really isn't so much a 'where' as a 'when,'" she replied. "I felt your need for me so powerfully that I surrendered to it, and here I am, but if you no longer need me, I'm not sure if I will be able to stay for long."

"I just died, or at least I went through the equivalent," I told her. "I wonder how the others feel."

"Their experience was real," she said, "Look."

In the wreckage of the aircraft, people were stirring. As I watched a middle-aged man stand up and stare around in terrified bewilderment, I remembered why I was here. This is what Seine's reference to finding out for myself was all about. Everybody on this plane had made an abrupt transition from physical life—to what? I guess it depended on their beliefs and conditioning.

I was recovering rapidly, and Treenie was still with me.

"Come on, let's help them," she said.

Together, we assisted the people who most needed us. Because there had been only nine people on board, including the pilot and navigator, we were able to give each person a lot of attention. Without exception, they were all deeply shocked by their abrupt death, and apart from the pilot, all were unable to come to terms with being so-called dead.

"How can I be dead?" one man wailed in a quavering tone. "I'm here, standing up, unhurt. How can I be dead?"

He was hysterical because he was staring, mesmerized, at his own torn and mutilated body. That it was dead was only too apparent.

"Geeoooorrgeeee!" The only female passenger was his wife, and she had just caught sight of his body. She seemed to ignore her own, still strapped into the torn-off seat. Apart from the fact that her head was sliced neatly off at the brow, with a lot of resulting blood and brains spilled out, she was unmarked. She could not relate to her body at all. "Geeeoooorrrrrgggggeee," she screamed, in a voice thick with horror.

"Oh God. Oh God. Oh God. Oh God," a younger man, maybe in his early twenties, repeated over and over. His metaphysical self seemed even younger than his body, but with his body turned practically inside out, it was an impression rather than a comparison.

Not all registered their shock in words. Two men sat side by side, staring at each other in stunned silence. Metaphysically, they could all see and hear one another; they were also aware of Treenie and me. Only the pilot seemed aware that he could not possibly have survived. "My wife had it right," he muttered. "I must be dead, yet I'm not dead."

To get them away from the trauma of their mutilated bodies, we helped them from the wreckage. They acted

129

as though they were still physical, stumbling and falling as we guided them to a clearing farther into the trees. This made a considerable difference. Comforting them, Treenie embraced them all in powerfully visualized Light.

We must have crashed very close to a town, for with a blast of sirens, two ambulances came onto the scene, emerging from a track among the trees. They quickly and efficiently began to deal with the bodies, picking up parts and placing them in identifiable piles. One young man went suddenly white and turned away gagging as he tried to untangle the inside-out body from the wreckage.

"All right, son. Take a few deep breaths. There's no rush. At least they aren't suffering." An older man looked around, his own face haggard. "Christ almighty! I've seen a few nasty ones in my time, but this caps it all. What a mess!"

The young man vomited, unable to prevent it. The air was hot, and thick with stink. Already a cloud of flies was swarming over the bodies.

Despite the young man's temporary setback, the team worked swiftly, and by the time fresh sirens announced the arrival of police, the fire brigade, more ambulances, and other helpers, the bodies and parts were laid out, ready for bagging and removal.

"Holy Mother of God!" The first policeman out of the car turned away, shuddering. "Every time I see something like this it reminds me of how bloody vulnerable we are. Our bodies are as soft as jelly babies."

I dismissed the work on the physical scene, for in some ways it had complicated matters. George had seen the ambulance men and wanted to go with them. He was convinced he needed medical attention. The fact that his body was dead had not yet penetrated his consciousness, for he knew that he was alive.

"Isn't it ridiculous that people believe that they are their bodies. It never dawns on them that the death of a body is no more than that—not the death of the Being they are," I said to Treenie.

We had our work cut out with George, for although the others had become quiet and subdued in the shock of abrupt transition, George was hyperactive.

With sudden inspiration, I visualized the Lady Gold, and I called to her in my consciousness. She was with us instantly. Walking over to George, she touched his brow, and he calmed immediately. Without appearing to glance at what we were doing, she spoke to us.

"You have done very well. The abrupt disruption of a person's reality is not easy to assimilate, especially when that person has the usual human attachments. Metaphysical hysteria is just as real as physical hysteria."

She looked at us both intently. "I see now why you are here. Words could not convey this experience; neither could passively witnessing it. You each experienced this in the way that pertains to your pattern of growth."

She grinned at me. "You always were a glutton for trauma." She and Treenie shared a conspiratorial smile.

"Just a minute," I protested. "This wasn't my idea; it was . . . " My words tailed off. Of course I was responsible for where I was and what I experienced. Everybody is, but very few accept or acknowledge it. Far easier to blame!

"Well, it was a very powerful lesson," I said lamely.

Treenie came over and kissed me. I closed my eyes with a sigh. "That's just what I need," I said, but as I went to hug her, she vanished. The Lady Gold summoned other Light workers to help her, and . . .

. . . I, too, was back in the reality of the vast, open hospital in a metaphysical realm.

Seine gazed at me, quiet and serious.

"That was not nice," I said mildly.

He smiled his approval and barely hidden relief.

"And what did you learn?"

"That not *all* lessons need to be learned the hard way!"

7

No Earthly Hospital

There is a halfway house
in which the weary rest.
Their exhaustion stems
not from conquest, but conflict;
not wholeness, but isolation;
not the truth of Self, but self-deceit.

"So what *did* you learn?"
"Never to trust the smile of a sphinx."
"Be serious, Michael."
"Whatever makes you think I'm not serious?"
"You are being unnecessarily flippant."
"Actually, you're wrong. Now that it's all over, I'm so shaken that I could cry endlessly."
"Why?"
"Because humanity lives in a framework of belief that is totally inappropriate for today's reality. If the general public had the faintest idea of the truth of Self and the continuity of life, an accident like that would have had a very different outcome. The reaction and fear those people experienced in the death of their bodies affected Treenie and me. That's why. Their fear and pain was our hurt also."
"Don't ever suggest again that you lack compassion."
"In fact, there would be no accidents," I continued. "What our personal self calls an accident, our soul Self

134

knows as purpose. Accidents fit the belief of separation and blame, but their reality is purpose."

"And their purpose?"

"To consciously experience Oneness as a reality."

With a look of satisfaction on his face, Seine led me through the gardens. We walked across some beds of creeping, short-stemmed, yellow flowering plants that seemed to welcome our footsteps, and on toward a small lake. When we reached the rock-fringed edge of the water, I followed my impulse and waded in, swimming into the tranquil coolness.

It was a healing. Soothing energies flowed through me in accordance with my movement through the water. The water seemed normal, yet it felt alive and involved in my action of swimming in it. A fast-flowing river or stream interacts with a swimmer, but calm lakes are normally passive. This lake had the character of a fast-flowing stream, with the added ability to heal inner trauma.

When I emerged, all trauma was resolved. I wish it could be as easy for those nine victims as it is for me, I thought. I must have broadcast the thought, for Seine continued with it.

"We can visit them now if you like."

For a moment, I resisted. The thought of more of George was not all that appealing, but I knew that I would like to see him and the others as they recovered. Would the experience change their view of life? Would they still hold onto the illusions of their previous beliefs? Could they accept a new reality?

"Okay. Where are they?"

As he reached out to touch my shoulder, I realized that another place shift was involved.

"But aren't they here?" I asked.

"No. They are at a place you would call a halfway house. They need an integration process before they come here. Or *if* they come here. There are many other such healing centers. Incidentally, the pilot is not with them. He always expected that a crash would end his life, and with his wife he had studied metaphysical concepts for years. Now that the concepts are reality, he made the transition easily." Seine touched my shoulder briefly, and . . .

✳

. . . we were elsewhere. A large brick building faced us, very much like a comfortable and familiar private nursing home, but with a touch of real class. I noticed Seine trying not to smile too obviously.

"So what's the joke?"

"I am aware of the way you see the halfway house. It appears to different people in a way that they feel comfortable and safe with."

I tried to be outrageous. "You mean if I felt happiest and safest in an English pub, that is what I would see?"

"Exactly."

We walked into an atmosphere of love, care, and service. I felt as though a cocoon of safety enclosed me, and I *knew* that nothing in the wide world could ever frighten or threaten me again.

"Does every patient feel this? Do you?" I asked.

Seine nodded. "It is nourishing, isn't it? Such an immea-surable embrace of love."

Of course, it really was different from my nursing home image. There was no reception to tell us visiting hours, no one to tell us where to go or not go. I only had to focus my thoughts on George and his companions, and we were with them. Now that's what I call room service!

To my utter astonishment, George recognized me.

"Hey, guys! It's the other fellow who was on the plane." He turned to me. "What a crash! Christ! I don't know how we survived it. Glad you made out okay." He gestured all around us. "Great place this—wonderful service—but they won't let any relatives or friends visit. Can't understand that."

I looked at Seine, speechless. Well, almost! "He thinks he is still alive," I said softly.

"Hey, buddy! Who the hell are you talking to! There's only us in here."

Seine had such a huge smile I could see the blue rows of vestigial teeth. I was surprised to see that there were several rows! His species must have been effective carni-vores back in their beginnings.

Silently, Seine corrected me. "Don't judge me on the history of your planet. We were never carnivores." I felt his mental image of a shudder at the thought.

"Can't you see anyone else?" I asked George.

"How could I?" George replied indignantly. "There's no one else to see." He looked at me as though I had a problem!

"This reality automatically screens the patient," Seine continued in his silent projection. "If the patients were my species in their primitive past, it's you who would probably be invisible. Now, let's see you try and introduce George to a more expanded reality. You asked for this!"

I groaned silently. Me and my big mouth! "George, have you considered how strange it is that you were not killed in that plane crash?"

George had an easy answer. "Bloody miracle, that's what! Poor old Bert had both legs broken and his collarbone all smashed up, but they work bloody marvels in this place. He's as good as new already."

I looked at Seine despairingly. My God! Talk about illusions. I knew what had happened. To protect their belief systems, George and the others had rationalized their way through, and as they believed and projected, so it became. We do create our own reality—alive or dead!

I walked over to the other patients, greeting them and being greeted. Without exception, all believed that they were alive in their old bodies, and none saw anything that could not be rationalized.

I looked at Seine. "I quit," I said in a clear, firm voice.

George looked startled. "What do you mean, you quit? And who the hell are you talking to? There's no one over there."

"You are wrong, George. A friend of mine is standing here with us, but you can't see him. You know why?" My voice had become forceful. "Because you are so limited, that's why. Because your belief system is so fragile you can't embrace anything new or expansive. The fact is, George, you and all your friends here are physically dead."

George looked rather like a stranded fish, and his mouth

opened and closed several times before his words gushed out.

"Ho, buddy boy! I think you got banged around in that crash more than you realize. You must have hit your head."

I sighed and walked over to a guy named Ralph. He was a small, middle-aged man who looked as if he might be a bit more sensitive than George.

"Ralph, can you describe your nurse?"

"Sure," he beamed. "Really angelic. A woman about my age, slim, and somehow shrouded in light." He looked startled. "I mean, *really* angelic!"

"Don't be soft, Ralph." The speaker was the slim young man. "Our nurse looks just like Michelle Pfeiffer. A real knockout!"

"Come on, Mick, that's not right," George interrupted. "She isn't angelic either. Matter of fact, she looks just like my mum."

"Funny you should say that, George," Bert said, as he joined in. "I reckon she's the spitting image of my sister Betty. She used to be a nurse."

By now they were beginning to look both bewildered and apprehensive. But I had not quite finished.

"Okay, George," I said. "Describe this room you are in."

"It isn't a room; it's a hospital ward."

"Oh! What color are the walls?"

George looked at me pityingly. "Christ, you did get hurt. I reckon you're in the wrong place, buddy."

"What color, George?"

"Green, of course. A pale lime green."

Ralph looked startled all over again. "Come on, George.

Don't be daft. The whole room is painted a soft rose pink. I should know, I grow roses that exact color. And it ain't a ward. This is a large, comfortable lounge room."

"Rubbish! They are lime green walls, the color of my living room, and it's a hospital ward."

"Actually, you are both wrong." The speaker this time was an older, rather mild-mannered man. "The walls are all papered with a pattern of floral bouquets. My favorite aunt used to have this pattern in her parlor. I always loved it. In fact, this *is* her parlor."

The group was now staring at one another in astonishment.

"You each see that which gives you the most comfort and security," I told them. "Your nurse, the room, and its furnishings, etcetera. We could go on and on with this, and I doubt that you would agree on anything."

I paused, giving them time for all this to sink in.

"Don't you think that if you were all physically alive, you would all see the same nurse and the same room?"

George was ever vocal, but the bluster had gone. "But . . . but . . . if we were killed, how can we still be alive?"

I decided to keep it simple. "Because death is really the death of your physical body. But you are *not* your body, as you have just discovered. You are a soul that continues forever. You have just left your familiar three-dimensional reality. Do you really believe you could all have survived that horrific plane crash?"

"Just supposing you're right," a subdued George said. "If we are physically dead, what happens next?"

"That's entirely up to you."

"Well, what should we do?" Ralph asked.

"What would you like to do?"

"I would like to know who *you* are," Mick said. "Are you dead? And if you are, how come you know about it and we don't?" He looked suddenly stricken. "We ain't in that other place, are we?"

I laughed. "Rest assured you are in *your* version of heaven, or at least on the way there. As for me, I'm just a wandering soul learning a few lessons, and I'm not dead. The only reason you saw me after the crash was because you were physically dead. I was there nonphysically, just as I am now."

"How can you be nonphysical? I can see you as large as life," George protested.

"That's because you are nonphysical also."

George slapped his leg with a loud whack. "That's real, buddy," he said emphatically.

With a sigh, I resorted to theatrics. Waving my hand through his leg, I passed it up through his body. George yelped and leapt about a yard into the air.

"For Christ's sake! How the hell did you do that?"

"Just showing you that you're not quite as solid as you seem to think," I said, grinning hugely. This was getting to be fun! "I can accommodate your vibrational pattern."

I noticed Seine frowning at me, while trying to hide a smile. I figured I'd better wind it up.

"Humor me," I suggested. "Let's just suppose you are no longer physically living. Of all the people you know who are dead, George, who would you most like to be with right now?"

He did not hesitate. "My mum."

"Okay, George, now concentrate on her. See her in your mind's eye, and call her." I looked around at the others.

"Each of you, visualize someone you love who is no longer alive, and call out to him or her in your thoughts. Ask him or her to come to you."

Eyes were screwed up as they all concentrated. After a while, George glanced around. "There's no one here," he said, looking disappointed.

"Go and open the door to your ward, George," I suggested. "And why don't you others go with him."

Hesitant, they all walked over to the door. Hanging back, they seemed loath to open it. Either way, it would be a challenge. If their relatives were there, that meant they were dead, and if they weren't there, that carried its own disappointment. Finally, squaring his shoulders, Ralph gently opened the door.

A small group of people came in and began embracing the men who had called to them. For Ralph, it was the angelic nurse, his late and beloved wife. George was crying softly in the arms of his mother, once again being comforted as though a child. Sisters, brothers, mothers, wives, and aunts—all were reunited. The real healing would now begin. I knew it was time for Seine and me to depart, but for moments longer I wanted to just witness the triumph of love in that room as the men accepted their fate and a changed reality.

"What about George's wife?" I asked.

Seine pointed to a woman who had come in with the group.

"Despite her initial hysteria, she assimilated her physical death quickly and easily. It seems that she has long held a secret belief in the continuity of the soul and an afterlife."

"What a stupid term—afterlife," I said. "This is not 'after' life. How can it be if life continues? If people thought in terms of 'everlife' it would make more sense."

Seine smiled at me. "That may well come about, Michael, but I must say you did very well in here. A bit direct and confrontational, but not without compassion. And it was certainly very effective."

We disappeared from the halfway house just as George called out, "Hey, buddy, I want . . . "

❋

I was standing near the lake of the metaphysical hospital with Seine, those last fading words lingering in my mind. I wonder what he wanted?

"Thanks, Seine, that was great! Being a part of their expanding reality was quite something. Now I understand the role of the Lady Gold far better, except that she works in the fresh trauma of it all. What happens to George and the group now?"

"Exactly as you said; it's up to them. Probably they will come to a healing center like this for a brief while, but in the end it is their conditioned subconscious beliefs that will construct their continuity."

"Does that always mean more of a false belief in separation, with more of its attendant fear, suffering, and pain when they incarnate back into an Earth reality?"

143

Seine looked sad. "Usually, until Truth prevails. It is Truth that sets you free."

We sat on a lakeside rock to talk. "I suppose a person who dies hating and angry has a hard time," I mused.

"There are many who never see the Light before they are back in another body to repeat the old patterns of habitual revenge—and thus more suffering. It never ceases to amaze me that the greatest human habit is an attachment to pain and suffering. The human subconscious is saturated in it."

Following a cue from Seine, we walked toward a building that shone forth with radiant light. Even as we approached, I could feel a purity of spirit as though great Beings dwelt here.

"This is a very special place, not unique, for there are others, but all are of a high, fine vibration. This is where many advanced souls come at their moment of transition."

"Are we allowed in?" I asked.

Seine laughed. "Any place here that you can enter, you are allowed in. It is your own Beingness that determines it. Would you like to go in?"

I nodded, and with some trepidation I walked into the high, arching entrance. I almost expected to be unable to enter, but I passed easily beneath the living portals of flowering stone. It is difficult to describe the interior, for once again, the details related to the occupant in whatever way that most pertained. What Seine saw, I can't image, but for me it was more like the interior of a huge botanical greenhouse than anything else, but also luxuriously furnished. What really impressed me was the fact that however differently Seine and I might experience the interior, our realities were perfectly synchronized as we strolled along.

As I admired a clambering mass of gloriosa lilies in full red and yellow magnificence, a human Being gradually materialized nearby.

She looked around, a smile of delight lighting her features as she recognized her surroundings. "Oh, glory be! Back again." Then she saw me. "Oh, how clever. You are here, yet you are still physically alive." She looked at me inquiringly.

Her powers of perception took me by surprise.

"Well, yes. I'm just a visitor, but how did you know? Is it that obvious?"

She laughed, a quiet chuckle of contentment. "Oh yes, my dear. It's very obvious. Your companion, for example, has not had a physical body — in human terms — for a long time. But you, even in this metaphysical state, carry your physical aura."

I felt a huge sense of relief, of immense gratitude, toward this wonderful woman, and she immediately knew it.

"Why do you feel so much gratitude?" she asked.

I told her about the aircraft accident and my involvement. "I feel a profound sense of relief to know that people like yourself are also involved with humanity, that we are not all totally ignorant about life and death."

She smiled at me, and I felt bathed in light.

"Your relief is a measure of your compassion. In every age, Truth has its expression, and in every age it reaches its peak. We are approaching a peak of Truth. But as in all natural balance, the opposite is also true. The illusions of life also have their peak simultaneously."

"How would you identify the two pinnacles?" I asked. "And how do we reach them?"

"It is all to do with focus. If you focus on your spiritual Self, you reach the peak of Truth. If material wealth and possessions are your focus, you reach the peak of life's illusions. In our present times, each person makes his or her choice."

"Yes," I replied, "but the real irony is that not choosing is also a choice—the choice of self-denial. There is no neutral ground. We are always climbing one pinnacle or the other. By the way, where did you come from as you materialized here?"

"Why, Earth, of course. My physical body died as I appeared here."

"You mean you just let go and here you are?"

"Yes. That says it nicely. I was quite elderly, and I knew very clearly that my life's purpose was finished. So I gave my loved ones some of my little treasures, tidied up my affairs, and left my body."

"What! Just like that? You mean you dropped dead?"

She laughed. "Not quite. I died in my sleep. I organized to come to a center like this as I dreamed, knowing that the dream was fabricated from reality. Then, with clear knowing, I departed my body."

"It's that simple?"

"Of course, if you are aware. If you know that who you are is not born and never dies, what is there to cling to? Life's continuity is our truth, not death and endings."

I hugged her, grinning at Seine. "This is just what I needed. This is wonderful."

After more conversation, we each went our own way — Seine and I further into the building, the woman out into the gardens. As she departed, she was leaping around like an exuberant child. "I am just enjoying real freedom of movement again," she called out. "Isn't it delightful?" She pirouetted before us in a gust of light. "Human bodies are so terribly limited, especially with gravity." She was now spinning into the air, weightless, laughing at her own unintended joke.

"What an absolutely lovely person," I said, as we continued along an ongoing combination of small, crystal clear waterfalls and a meandering stream, all set into the most incredible landscaping — at least in my perception.

"Where are we going?" I asked.

"You have seen people being healed, and you have been involved in some healing. You have seen enough to realize that all healing is Self-influenced. Healers can only catalyze another's healing — and what a gift! You have also seen one who needed no healing, knowing her truth."

"Are you saying that where there is a true knowing of Self, there can be no sickness based on illusion?"

"Of course!" Seine looked surprised. "No discord."

"Yes, of course," I echoed. "I knew that, too, but somehow I lost sight of it."

"To continue with what I was saying," Seine said, "just as people arrive in various states of conscious awareness, so, too, they depart. You may be interested?"

"So where are we going," I joked, "a launching pad?"

"That is a fairly accurate description," he said seriously.

"Oh, really?"

I admit, I had several expectations of a departure lounge, somewhat like an airport, but what we came across as we left the indoor botanical garden took me by surprise. We walked onto a beautiful lawn, over which a number of hot-air balloons were hovering. They were about a foot off the ground, unstaked, and the flame that kept them inflated was completely silent.

I gazed around, flabbergasted. "Is this a joke?"

At that moment, a group of maybe twenty young people came across the lawn toward us. They were laughing and chattering in great excitement. "Hello there," a young man called out, approaching me. It became apparent that he saw only me. I knew that I would have to play along with the charade.

"Coming for a ride, are you?"

"No. I'm just watching."

"Great morning for a ride. The weather's perfect. We all got up at four to catch this breeze at daybreak."

It was most odd. For me, this was a spherical time frame, certainly not early morning. Also I felt no breeze at all, yet it was ruffling his hair. Very clearly, we experienced different realities here.

"Do you know where you are?" I asked the cheerful young man.

"Funny you should ask that. We were drifting across an African desert when we got caught in a twister. You know, a whirlwind. For a few moments, there was total pandemonium." He paused, frowning, looking puzzled. "You know,

I could have sworn that most of us were thrown out and that the balloons were torn to shreds. I recall a terrifying sensation of falling, but I must have imagined it. Anyway, the next thing we knew, we were all sharing a ward in this incredible hospital." He grinned, a fresh and likable smile banishing his frown. "Talk about wonderful nurses. So, here we are, all our broken bones mended and ready to continue our flight."

"This is Africa?"

He looked as surprised as I felt. "Of course! Where else would it be? This hospital is in Nairobi, Kenya."

I looked at Seine helplessly, and he shook his head.

"Well, have a nice flight," I said. "Pretty good technology, huh? Silent flames!"

He looked at me as though I were mad. "Good technology?" he echoed. "I can hardly hear you above the noisy flare of the flames. Well, good-bye."

He offered me his hand, and as I shook it, I solemnly intoned, "May all your twisters be little ones."

As the laughing, chattering group clambered into the hot-air balloons, their energy radiated an essence of great innocence and purity.

I turned to Seine. "If I didn't see this, I would not believe it. They all think that they are physically alive and in Africa!"

"That's true, Michael, but there is another important factor as well. Despite their attachment to a mass illusion—which is very, very common—they are here in this very pure vibration. Ignorance did not prevent it."

"I know what you mean," I offered. "They have a wonderful intent and purpose in life. There is no malice or hate in them. No anger or real discord. They are a caring, loving bunch of people enmeshed in an illusion. So what happens next? Are we involved?"

"No, this is where we leave them. I wanted you to see yet another state of being. I can assure you that their flight is going to take them through a powerful learning process about truth, for this is what they are invoking on a soul level."

I felt relieved and happy for them. "I was joking about the launching pad, you know."

"And I thought you were being perceptive!"

We wandered away from the lawn, heading into an area of flowering plants. "Do you see flowers here?" I asked him.

"Actually, I do. Roses."

"But that's what I am seeing," I expostulated. Then I noticed that we were not alone. A small boy was holding the hand of an elderly man. They looked rather like grand-father and grandson. Seine and I walked over to them. As we approached, they seemed to blur for a moment and then to reappear as two men of indeterminate age. They both smiled at us in genuine pleasure.

"Well met, friends, well met," the darker of the two said. "My name is Raoul. This is Felix."

We shook hands, all formal and polite. If they noticed anything different about Seine, they did not show it.

"I realize that you saw us change age," Raoul said. "I would like to explain that. Felix and I died in an accident in the French Alps recently. In that incarnation, we were related: I, the grandfather, and Felix, my grandson. However, we are familiar with the illusion of incarnate life, and we are now in a more appropriate age and body relationship." He shrugged. "The human form can become a comfortable habit. We both enjoyed our role. But, as you obviously realize, our accident had a purpose. We had experienced all that was necessary in our relationship, so through purpose we acted in accord with a disastrous natural happening—a landslide."

He smiled wistfully. "We were momentarily extending that role in this garden of peace. Even the roses are named Peace."

I nodded. I had recognized them. "Do you have to incarnate back on Earth again?" I asked.

Felix looked at me keenly, and it was he who answered.

"Actually, no. We both know our truth. However, we are committed to helping humanity, especially in the existing conflict between material wealth and spiritual values. We will return, for as a soul-bonded pair we have much to offer those who search for Self."

"A soul-bonded pair! Can you explain what that means?"

Felix smiled kindly. "You will know its meaning soon enough. Its truth is an experience, not shared information."

"It's probably wishful thinking, but it's a pity that many of our religious leaders are unable to experience a greater truth," I said.

"Some do," Felix replied, "but most Western religions epitomize separation by worshiping a divine but separate deity. This literally separates Self from God, religion from truth."

Bidding them farewell, Seine and I walked toward an

area that seemed to shine with Light. As we drew nearer, I was surprised that there was no building or apparent source of the illumination.

"This is something special," Seine told me. "Because you are based in physicality, you will find a very definite limit on how far you can venture into this Light."

"But what is it? The feeling just on the outer fringe is incredible." I felt as though I was standing in the presence of some great and cosmic God. It was overwhelming. But what made it truly wonderful was a total absence of feeling belittled or insignificant. This Light uplifted and expanded all life within its influence. Under its influence, my insight and intuition flowered. I knew that all humanity is affected by the Light and that a focus on our spiritual Self magnifies its intensity.

Together, Seine and I walked—if that was the word, for within this Light I'm sure I floated—further into its heart. I came to a stop. I could not proceed any further. Neither I nor anything else stopped me, but it was my limit. Seine continued, vanishing. I felt utterly content. I knew that this Light was a focus of Love, the radiance of Love. Beyond that, I was content not to know.

In my easy acceptance of my limit, I suspect that I was given a gift. With my inner vision, I could see a small group of resplendent Beings coming into the Light, manifesting their energy of Being into its heart. Other Beings were leaving in a similar way, their Beingness swallowed in Light as they departed to other realms. The Beings were of Love, of Light. Beyond any shadow of doubt, I knew this to be our ultimate human reality: We are immortal Beings of Light.

I had not the vaguest concept of time, nor was there any. I might have been there a thousand linear years or a heartbeat, but when I turned and walked away, it was by my own volition.

I sat for a while, leaning against a tree just beyond the outer fringe of the Light. I knew it was eternal. Seine appeared from the gardens behind me. We just looked at each other. There was nothing to be said.

☀

My feeling of euphoria gradually dwindled, my awareness becoming focused on my physical body, sitting on numb and cramped legs as I leaned against the tree in the gully near our house.

The echidna was long gone, and I wondered briefly if it ever did realize I was there. I thought about all that had happened, taking my time to assimilate it, while stretching my legs with a stifled groan as pins and needles danced and pricked with the now unrestricted flow of blood. It was one of those moments when physical bodies seemed a bit of a drag. I looked at my watch. One hour had passed!

8

An Evolving Nature

Evaluate your focus in life.
For example, righting wrongs
judges and separates,
while acknowledging wholeness
uplifts and connects.

A lone in our house, I was sitting in my comfortable chair, thinking about which metaphysical reality I was about to enter. I decided to try for a change from the Temple of Learning or the cosmic hospital. After all, if I got to choose my experience, what was wrong with a bit of quiet exploring. I was getting ready to go Beyond once more, so I decided to set a clear image in my mind of what I wanted to experience. However, try as I might, no clear images would form. The harder I tried to focus on an imagined delight, the more vague and fuzzy it all became. I sighed. I had the feeling that once again the unknown and the unexpected would claim me. This, as always, forced me to rely on my Self.

I relaxed, releasing all sense of personal identity. As my focus gradually lost all definition of self—of me or them, of here or there, and of the many wants—as everything became nothing, . . .

✳

. . . once again all my lurking expectations were shattered. "Hello, Michael. I knew that we would meet again soon." I had stepped straight into the Temple of Learning. Thane was there, welcoming me as I recovered from my surprise.

"Don't I get any control over my moments at all?" I asked after hugging Thane with genuine pleasure. Hugging in that reality is much more all-embracing than in Earth reality, but it means the same. Only then did I notice that Thane looked different. He seemed more ethereal, less substantial, more light, less body.

"Yes," he replied in his childlike way, "when you accept a greater vulnerability."

"I thought I was very vulnerable," I protested.

"You are, to a degree. I do not seek to belittle you, but despite your Self-awareness, you still subconsciously wear a fine chain-mail armor as a form of protection. You don't need it. Although it allows you freedom of movement, it also restricts you. You are aware that becoming free is the birth of purpose, but even a flexible restriction is a limit on the expression of both the freedom and the purpose."

"I didn't know that I was wearing subconscious armor," I said defensively.

"You have nothing to defend, Michael. The change you see in me is brought about by your own development. Do not forget that I am an aspect of Self."

"Really? I did that! Can I get rid of the chain mail and become more vulnerable?"

"Yes. Vulnerable, defenseless, and naked!"

Inadvertently, I projected my sudden thoughts of Saint Francis of Assisi at the moment of his Self-realization.

"Yes! His realization of this was so profound that he felt compelled to strip his body naked to implant forever the truth of being naked and vulnerable. If you believe that you need protection, then you do, for your own belief will create the need for it. In fact, it is this belief that will be the basis of any attack. Do you believe you need protecting?"

"No, I know I don't. As I said, I didn't even know I was protecting myself."

"Are you ready to become naked, Michael?"

As he finished speaking, I saw a single tear form in each of his eyes. What prompted me, I'll never know, but on impulse, I stepped forward and with my fingertips brushed the tears away from the corners of his eyes. In an impossible way, a single teardrop remained full and unbroken on one fingertip of each hand, and, again following the strange impulse, I put the teardrops to my mouth, touching them with my tongue. Instantly, I felt a searing pain shoot like a lightning bolt through my psyche—a pain that doubled me over and, as I collapsed, seemed to gather all the unresolved hurt of my foreverness into a single, choking sob.

It would be untrue to say I cried, but from the deepest recesses of my Being, the shaft of lightning purged my hurt in that one gasping cry. And I *knew* that it was the Light I had recently entered that had somehow released the hurt, lighting my innermost reaches.

As I got to my feet, in consciousness I stood naked before Thane. The formless, invisible chain mail that I had never realized existed had gone. I felt lighter, freer, more whole, and very vulnerable.

Thane looked delighted. "How wonderful it is to witness

the timing of truth. You now *realize* that you have nothing to defend, for truth needs no defense. You will find that vulnerability also contains its own blessings, for you are not born and you cannot die. Always be naked to Self, for in that utter acceptance you will find clarity and insight."

He looked at me solemnly. "You have now accepted your purpose, and I Am that purpose." With these words, he simply stepped into me and we were One.

I staggered slightly; it had all happened so smoothly. First White Bear, now Thane; this took a bit of getting used to.

Only moments ago, I had asked Thane when I would get control over my own movements; well, now I had it, for I was alone.

I looked around, trying to get my bearings. That I was in the Temple of Learning was the only certainty I had, for the high fluted ceiling that hovered just centimeters above sculptured pillars was familiar. Nevertheless, it was an area new to me, although I suspected that the interior of the Temple of Learning would always be new. Hesitantly, I walked down the center of a hallway, not having the faintest idea of where I was going or why. I had a vague wish to experience more of the consciousness of Nature— to gain a deeper insight into Nature's reality—but my thoughts were nebulous and undefined.

I continued for a while, walking on a white marble floor so pristine pure it felt as if no one had ever walked in here before. Insight revealed that the Temple of Learning erased all imprint of whoever entered, forever retaining its immaculate purity.

159

Because the Temple of Learning does not relate to normal experience, it is difficult to describe the impression that my walk, while revealing nothing, was taking me through many possible realities. And because I was in spherical time, I had no idea how long that walking continued, or even if I ever moved from the one place.

There was a moment, however, when I saw what looked like a small, transparent bubble floating in the air some distance ahead of me. My footsteps appeared to bring us closer, although I soon discovered that it had its own means of locomotion. Only an arm's length away, it hovered about chest height in front of me; I was filled with an instant recollection. I had dreamt about this Being many times. I now knew that it was one of the Beings of whom I had inner knowledge, but knowledge that had long been inaccessible. Because of the dreams, this Being was familiar to me and welcome.

I faced a perfect globe, maybe a yard in diameter; it was transparent and filled with a colorless liquid gas. Suspended in the liquid was what appeared to be a plant, but what a plant! It was a fist-sized bulb, capped with a foliage of iridescent, moving shards of light. It was a Being of ethereal beauty; but far more than that, it was intelligent! "You are so wonderful." My silent projection of admiration came from me unwittingly.

"I am a Wonder-Neap. That is the closest translation possible. Would you like to journey with me?"

"I have dreamt about you so many times that I feel I know you. Each time I feel an incredible connection, but as I reach out to touch you, invariably I wake up."

"Or perhaps you fall asleep! Would you like to journey with me?"

"I would consider it a privilege."

The Wonder-Neap's foliage waved delicately in the liquid, while prisms of rainbow light danced within the globe. I had the sudden insight that this rainbow light was food for the wondrous plant, and that it was self-perpetuating in some form of natural, symbiotic relationship.

"You have dreamt of wanting to touch me, and you may now do so. But first, I will touch you."

For a brief moment, the Wonder-Neap opened its consciousness, metaphysically touching me, and an incredible wave of transcendent intelligence engulfed me. It was so far beyond my human experience that I was dazed, but any vague remnants in my conditioning that conferred intelligence to people and none to plants was totally annihilated.

In turn, I reached out my hand and touched the Wonder-Neap, and . . .

❋

. . . everything changed, even the familiar Earth of my normal reality. As I gazed around, I realized that this was a very early era on a much younger Earth. Great swamps covered the land, with only the hills and ridges above water. It was cool, with no tall vegetation to be seen. Large flat, soft-leafed plants grew in abundant profusion in the shallow water and mud—mud that continuously oozed and bubbled as gases formed and escaped. There were a few animals to be seen, but they were generally of a reptilian shape, yet they also had a fishy look about them. Most were able to move efficiently in the water and on the land. Some seemed to be all teeth, long, sharp and formidable, while others were adapted for eating the lush plants. I saw nothing that had a thick, scaly skin or armor plating, or even any sign that such would develop. The animals had some resemblance to how one might imagine land sharks—not crocodiles—with the same lack of a definite skeleton, limbs, or bones.

I got so involved in my observation of this incredible prehistoric Nature that I committed a careless oversight. A nearby toothy predator had been sliding through the shallow water toward a rather large plant-eating species. When it made a final rush, the wicked needle teeth sinking into the gulping beast, a rapid, slithering, sliding, rolling, biting, hissing, heaving mass of prehistoric flesh and fury engulfed me. I was flattened, smashed down into the water, while a rage of beastial ferocity pressed me deeper and deeper into the oozing mud.

For long, horrendous moments I choked and gasped, the mud and muck dominating all inner knowing. I was lost in panic when a huge, heavy cartilaginous tail smashed into my head, and I sank into oblivion.

I opened my eyes to a brilliant blue sky that has also become extinct on Earth. It had a color and clarity of unbelievable depth. The Wonder-Neap hovered nearby, and if it was in the least concerned, I felt nothing. It emitted no emotions, no humor, no concern, nothing, yet I knew that it cared.

"A good way to learn a lesson."

And it was succinct! "What happened? How?"

"You forgot you are not physical."

It was true. I *had* forgotten I was not physical. I had been so rapidly overwhelmed during the struggle that I had jerked back into old physical reactions of fear, and for a while, they became my reality. Once I blacked out, my metaphysical Self resolved it, all physical illusions ending. A bit like life, I thought reflectively.

"Exactly! Good lesson."

"Did you know that would happen?" I asked.

Without replying, the Wonder-Neap hovered close, and everything changed again.

This was Earth of a later prehistoric time frame, with a climate and vegetation that left me gasping. I have experienced high humidity in the tropics, but this was like being in a sauna. The air was saturated heat, while the vegetation was beyond a botanist's wildest dreams. Where I stood, the landscape was dominated by very large cycads, plants with dark, lush green fernlike foliage. Huge primitive trees grew in scattered groups, but I do not know whether they were massive tree cycads, tree ferns, or some type of palm unknown to me. There was no grass, or any flowering plants, other than the cycads and club moss. This grew in a dense profusion, covering all the soil between and around the cycads. It was a lush, moist, verdant green. Physically, I would have had difficulty walking more than a few yards, so abundant was the vegetation.

Two other things that surprised me were the smell and the noise. The smell was astonishing. I could smell the wet soil and rotting vegetation as a pungent, overpowering odor of humus and decay. I liked it. It was the smell of a raw and pure Nature. I can only liken the noise to the sound of crickets and cicadas, except it was far louder than any I have ever heard physically. Despite my efforts to detect just one culprit, it was lost in the overall cacophony of sound. The club moss seethed with huge millipedes, centipedes, and other insect life, while the cycads seemed to house the insects responsible for the noise.

The Wonder-Neap hovered close by, floating with all the ease and grace of a helium-filled balloon. "You are perfectly safe," it projected silently. I was puzzled by its words until I saw the dinosaur. There is no way to describe the impact of such an awesome creature. I have stood in zoos admiring the elephants, impressed by their size, power, and majesty. But compared with what confronted me, an elephant had all the impact of a mouse. This creature towered above me. It seemed impossible that it could have moved this close without my hearing it, despite the background orchestra. Even more than its size, the impact came from its colossal presence.

I stared in mute awe. Although I now felt safe in my metaphysical state, the memory of my recent episode compelled me to take a few hasty steps back. Even the Wonder-Neap, which, I suspect, perceived life in a way that was far superior to vision, projected a feeling of awe. I was very relieved that the dinosaur was plainly vegetarian. It opened a vast mouth and cropped those huge, tough, four-meter-high cycads as easily as a cow crops grass. The thought of a carnivorous behemoth that could eat this way made me shudder. At a guess, this creature could have looked into the window on the third floor of a house, and its neck was not all that long, compared to its body. It was not without defense, for it was armor plated, with a huge, knobby swelling on the end of its tail that was a very effective club. One swipe with that would smash a car flat! Surprisingly, it moved with none of the crashing blunder that its massive size would suggest. It had a definite grace of movement, and it made no sound above the din in the background. As it grazed, it disturbed small reptilian creatures that darted from the undergrowth, running on their hind legs with remarkable agility and speed. None were longer than about two yards, with some considerably smaller, but all had a mouthful of sharp teeth. I looked at the Wonder-Neap, perplexed. As fantastic as all this was, I knew there had to be a purpose. What was it?

The Wonder-Neap was clearly attuned to my thoughts, for at that moment, it came closer. The globe very gently touched my light-body head, and my visual perception expanded and changed. I could now see the consciousness of the dinosaur. This was a shock. For such an immense creature, its consciousness was quite small, as though it were a misfit. I perceived consciousness as a shroud of illumination, completely independent of the body but in juxtaposition to it. When, at that moment, a few more of the small reptilian creatures ran from beneath the cycads, I was further surprised to see that their consciousness was far larger in proportion than that of their giant cousin.

"Consciousness draws to its Self form through which to express. When form can no longer extrapolate a greater physical potential, consciousness withdraws." The words were from the Wonder-Neap, and with them came understanding. The huge dinosaurs had grown progressively larger and larger over many millions of years, reaching their physical limit. As their physical bulk was becoming less and less appropriate for survival, consciousness was withdrawing from their vast bodies. The consciousness of the fast, agile reptilian creatures was still developing, as their potential grew and flourished. I was witnessing the evolution of consciousness through physical form.

Suddenly, everything went horribly wrong. A searing bolt of pure energy flashed past us, and I caught a glimpse of some Gray Beings standing on a cluster of nearby rocks. My mind a whirl, I dived for cover. What was happening? Had we been shot at?

I looked around for the Wonder-Neap. An envelope of shimmering light emanated from the globe; then I heard its silent words, "I will get help."

When it took off, it vanished in a flash of light. I crouched down, completely at a loss. Another lightning bolt of energy lanced past me, and ducking down in the undergrowth, I quickly changed my location. Was I the target, or was I simply in the way? So far, all the Beings I had encountered were benevolent. Were these hostile?

My attitude changed, and I took action. How or whether I could be injured in my light body, I had no idea, but I was never good at being passive. I needed to act. I had to find out what was happening and why.

Running in a fast crouch, I circled the rocks, coming up behind them. There were four humanoid Gray Ones, each standing about four feet tall. They were stout and pudgy, with muddy gray skins and a drab gray uniform. They did not feel nice, yet neither did they feel dangerous. I intuitively knew that they intended no serious harm but were more like a group of bully boys, and I lost my residue of fear. Their posture indicated that they were obviously arrogant, as they stood openly on the rocks as though impervious to anything I might do.

My earlier increased perception came to my aid, for I knew that I could tune into them, intuiting their intent. I remained behind them, keeping hidden, while they still faced the area I had vacated. Clever they might be, but intelligent?

As I focused on them, tuning in, an inner knowing unfolded. Although I was witnessing a prehistoric period, the Gray Ones are still with humanity to this day. I could not say I felt they were bad, any more than humanity is good, but their intent toward us is not for our benefit. Their energy felt strongly negative and, with a faint shock, I realized that they were able to project this negativity at people who had a similar focus. A person who focused on personal power and the manipulation of others was potential prey for the Gray Ones. They are attracted to such people, helping them to satisfy their desires while feeding off the resulting psychic negativity. They are not out to take control of our affairs, but to covertly influence us toward our basest and most negative desires.

The Gray Ones know that humans are truly Beings of Light. Their purpose seems to be to divert us from focusing on this truth, for when we focus on our Lightness, they

167

are powerfully repelled. Their real strength is in projecting the illusions of gain to be found in power, manipulation, and wealth. And humanity is an easy prey. However, just as the Gray Ones focus on the fear and negativity in humanity, so, too, that focus suppresses their own greater potential.

On impulse, I tried an experiment. As powerfully as I could, I visualized Light and Love encompassing them. The effect was startling. Within moments, they looked agitated and uncomfortable. I found it easy to do this, for I felt no enmity or anger toward them. I imagined Light in copious clouds illuminating the area around them, and their agitation became acute.

Within moments, they hurried to a small, silvery gray, disc-shaped craft, entered through a small opening that vanished when they were all in, and took off vertically. The craft disappeared with an instant, stupendous speed that reverberated with the crack of thunder.

Only as I stood alone, all action finished, did I begin to wonder about the Wonder-Neap. I realized that the Wonder-Neap could have taken me from any danger in an instant. I knew the Gray Ones were thoroughly unpleasant, but had I been set up? Walking to the warm, slightly steaming rocks in the ultratropical heat, I awaited my strange, multidimensional friend.

Another craft materialized nearby. It did not come from the sky; it simply appeared. Not only that, it did not look as though it could fly, being a large, circular sphere with a hazy spin to it. I knew, clearly, that these were "the good guys." Simultaneously, the Wonder-Neap appeared, almost seeming to grow from the air before me, so silent and instantaneous was its arrival.

"You learn faster than anticipated."

The comment was simple enough, but from the Wonder-Neap, it was rare praise. I felt good.

The spherical craft now dematerialized, revealing three Blue Beings who regarded me intently. Instantly, I recognized them. They were the Blue Beings I had recently visited in their city of fabulous, living spun glass. They, too, were humanoid, slightly smaller than I was, with fine, delicate bodies. Their skin was a deep blue, yet it had a translucent clarity very unlike human skin. Whereas the Gray Ones radiated negative energy, to a far greater degree the Blues emanated love and a deep sensitivity.

One of the Blue Beings projected silently: "As you have surmised, you were never in danger. The situation was unexpected, but we utilized it to observe how you would respond. With intuition and intelligence, you acted commendably."

I felt pleased. "I'm amazed that a prehistoric period should be so active with nonworldly Beings. Is this usual?"

"Both we and the Gray Ones can accommodate your linear time, appearing in any 'when' that is appropriate. In a greater reality, your past, present, and future all occupy the same spherical moment."

"Does that mean I could learn about our future?"

There was a hesitation. "Yes, it is possible, but only as a probability. Nothing in any measure of time is absolute. You would gain more confusion than clarity from such an exercise."

I thought about my next question carefully. "I learned about the Gray Ones by tuning in to them. The fact that you came to assist me suggests you are some kind of cosmic counterbalance?"

"You could say that. The Gray Ones try to negate other Beings. Humanity is not their only target. We seek to support those who focus on their spiritual integrity and love." I saw a whimsical smile on the features of the Blue Being who was communicating with me. "Generally, the people we aid are unaware of this. We do not manipulate people; we support them with a projected love and inspiration. Unlike the Gray Ones, we do not appear physically in your dimension. Although it is possible, it is extremely uncomfortable."

I grinned. "You're 'the good guys,'" I joked.

All three looked amused. "We do not relate to life in terms of good or bad. We are attracted to those Beings who seek to express their greatest potential of unconditional love. The Gray Ones play with shadows. Their own enlightenment is delayed while they play in the darkness of their own negativity. They seek to involve other races in their games of self-deception, thriving on the negative emotions that are invoked. However, they are unable to influence any humans who focus on their spiritual growth. The Gray Ones are not comfortable with Light and Love, as you discovered."

"Were you watching?"

"Watching is not the correct term. We . . . embraced the situation. We wished to observe how you would behave. We could have altered your reality instantly had there been a need to do so."

"Who are you? Where do you come from?" I asked.

"There are many people on Earth who know of us. It is generally accepted that we come from the Pleiadean group."

"Which is, of course, no answer at all."

"If the memory is not yet there, we deem it wisest not to invoke it. Once before, you had a dream experience of us that proved to be very unsettling. Be patient; allow this knowledge to emerge in natural timing."

During the conversation, the Blue Beings remained grouped together. One of them now touched a small gadget at its waist, and the spinning spherical craft reappeared, enclosing them. Very neat!

Although I could no longer see them, I felt a wave of love moving through my psyche. Silently I heard, "Our love is with you, always."

Just like that, they vanished.

The Wonder-Neap, who had remained silent throughout the exchange, was all brisk business. "We can now resume our intended purpose."

"Was our encounter with the Gray Ones arranged, or was it an accident?" I asked suspiciously.

"Nothing in life is accidental, nor are accidents possible. You know this. However, the encounter was not arranged."

I had to be content with this enigmatic reply! "Back to the evolution of consciousness," I quipped.

"Earth is going through a period of change. It is important that human emotional reactions are diluted by Truth," the Wonder-Neap informed me.

"Meaning?"

"Meaning that much of what seems to be happening on your planet is not all that it appears. This you will see."

Together, the Wonder-Neap and I wandered around on a prehistoric Earth. We traveled from one location to another, but all had a basic sameness, although I had another shock when I encountered a towering dinosaur of terrifying ferocity. This one was carnivorous, the type that killed and ate the monster vegetarian we saw earlier. It traveled fast, pacing the earth in a type of impatient bound that continually seemed to take other dinosaurs by surprise.

I saw it kill and eat a medium-sized creature, dispatching it with horrendous ease. Even though I was nonphysical, I kept well away. I found its efficiency at killing most disconcerting. I have admired the efficiency of cats and other modern predators, but this was very different. This was the furthest possible extreme of cold-blooded. There was a viciousness and ferocity involved in its killing that is now as extinct as the dinosaur, and I'm glad.

"Good insight."

With these words, I realized that with the passing of a species something else becomes extinct — the animal's expression that is not physical, but which its physical energy depicts. In the case of the carnivorous dinosaur — which I am sure was tyrannosaurus rex — it was an expression of killing. Vicious killing continues, but not in the way that *this* species of dinosaur expressed it. I now knew that with the passing of a biological era and its creatures, so, also, something of Nature that was no longer appropriate on Earth had passed. Only when the consciousness of the creature or plant concerned has reached its peak—not physically, but as consciousness—does the physical species begin its decline.

Under the Wonder-Neap's guidance, we began to make rapid shifts in time, but always with a purpose, as we followed the movement of consciousness. From a prehistoric age, we journeyed into other, more recent time frames. On one such occasion, we were somewhere in Europe in the late Middle Ages, emerging in the most wonderful, leafy forest. It was superb, the leaves caressing the soil in Nature's age-old ritual of love as a breeze stole through the branches. The sun seemed different from the one I am familiar with, but the difference was in the atmosphere. This was clean, the air amazingly fresh and pure; thus it altered the way I could see the sun. A nearby blast from a trumpet brought my attention to more immediate things. A couple of horsemen came at full gallop from under a vast oak tree, while racing in front of them was a mass of tangled animals. A loud, savage, raucous squealing rose from the din, smothered in the yelps, snarls, and growls of dogs.

As I stared, the animals briefly separated. A huge wild boar was flanked by five large hounds, all snarling teeth and menace. But it was the boar that held my attention. It was silent, apart from the sound it made as its foaming mouth chopped at the air. Tusks half the length of my forearm punched the air in warning as the head wove from side to side. Small, piggy eyes without a shred of fear danced with their own mad lust to kill, yet they missed nothing. And the creature was huge! The boar was as tall as a donkey and half again as wide—a fact that shocked me. It had long, shaggy hair covering its body, with a veritable mane from its ears to the middle of its back. I like pigs, and I kept a few large boars of my own when I had a piggery, but I had never imagined that their ancestry was such a bristling fury of savage death. This was truly a magnificent animal.

The horsemen were two sorry-looking specimens of humanity, dirty, coarse, and brutal. Under their urging, a couple of the dogs dashed in, one feinting left, the other right. Like a ballet dancer, the boar rose onto tiptoe, spinning to meet each with deceptive speed and ease. There was a thud, as the second dog was ripped and gored in seconds, while the first hung onto its grip at the top of a front leg. But only for moments. The boar reversed its spinning action, lifting the dog off the ground, before the tusks did their deadly work again.

The men held back. Armed with a lance and sword each, they were a cowardly pair.

"I tol' un were no use, unly the two un us." The words were a shout of anger and a curse.

The boar did not wait. It took off into the forest, pursued by dogs and riders, but I was certain that it would escape.

"It escapes men now, but not fate."

The Wonder-Neap was right. The European wild pig is long extinct, and while pigs of today have an obvious similarity, this wild boar was a king among them. No description does justice to its unique stature and cunning ferocity.

"Did you recognize the energy?"

I was puzzled for a moment, pondering the question. *"Perceive;* don't *think."*

Ah! With a mild shock, I did recognize it. The consciousness of the wild boar was almost identical to the consciousness of the predator that had flattened me in the ooze and slime of long ago. Almost, but not quite. This was consciousness evolving. It was the same consciousness, but a far more evolved expression. It had embodied change, developed it, and was due to change again!

"Consciousness is never static."

With these words, our leapfrogging through the time frames of Nature speeded up. Gradually, my overall perception increased as I learned to focus on Nature as a Whole rather than on individual animals, and I began to perceive the flow and movement of the consciousness of species. I learned that while a species developed its physical possibilities, flourished, and then vanished, always the consciousness of that species was moving on, evaluating an ever-greater potential. Not only that, but the life and living of a species determined its next stage of physical evolution. Physical form ended and became extinct, but never the conscious expression of that animal or plant. Always and forever, consciousness continued.

The experience I had shared with Elm was reemphasized; Nature has no relationship with death. It is an illusion to which we are so totally dedicated we have become lost in our own self-deceit.

The jumping from one era in Nature to another continued. We were in modern America when we emerged in a Park filled with specimen trees and flowering plants.

A chipmunk popped out from the roots of a tree and raced across the grass to a large rock, vanishing with an impudent flip of its tail.

I recognized it. This was the same consciousness that had expressed itself in the colossal, prehistoric vegetarian creature I had encountered. But what a change! Then, it was massive and, though stealthy, was limited by sheer bulk. Now, it was small, fast, dexterous, and much more intelligent, and its consciousness was more developed, more appropriate to this present time. The biggest change, however, was the relationship between its consciousness and the physical form. Previously, the physical bulk was totally out of proportion to its relatively small illumination of consciousness. Now, the consciousness was larger than its physical size! In fact, the chipmunk is one of only a few animals and other species like this.

"So what happened to the tyrannosaurus?" I asked.

Nothing altered. We stayed in the same beautiful Park, watching people walk by who had no idea that a Wonder-Neap and a metaphysical human were close by. Attracted by a blaze of color, I wandered across the grass toward a bed of flowering plants. Just as I reached them, a tiny bird flashed in a spark of brilliance from a tree and, hovering on a blur of wings before a flower, sipped the nectar.

"Oh yes!" I shouted in glee to the Wonder-Neap. This was the tyrannosaurus millions of years later: a hummingbird! Very changed, yet much of its nature remained. The ferocity of many species of hummingbirds is legendary in their territorial defense. And what a wonderful change from eating flesh to sipping nectar; from two legs that bounded along in a huge lumbering rush to two wings that are unique in their flight ability; from the huge bulk of its previous form to the agile wonder of today. And once again, that which had been tyrannosaurus rex now had a consciousness that was larger than its form—the very opposite of its former expression.

"Good. Your perception improves."

I smiled. The Wonder-Neap was not talkative, but it was certainly patient! We had been zipping around through millions of years of linear time just so I could learn to see the Whole from an overview, rather than remain lost in the introspective view of a deceptive and isolated reality.

We were off again, but we now stayed with modern time. We visited a school of pilot whales beached on the sand, dumped in their confusion at the height of a wild storm on a lonely windswept beach. I wept inside as I watched them threshing the sand helplessly, and I gasped when I realized that they were aware of us. Communication began as the whales died, for, like us, their physical bodies dictated their fear. As they died, no longer chained by fear, consciousness expanded.

"As with all life, we, too, submit to the evolution of spirit. Our bodies are large, and our medium very capable of this, but change is sweeping the planet Earth and nothing can remain unaffected. Our physical death is involuntary, for as you know, physicality clings to its dominance. However, when we emerge into the lighter, less dense ethers of spirit, we acknowledge our Truth. Does humanity do this?"

I sighed. "No. We cling to illusions, to self-deceit."

"But you know your own Truth. Why, therefore, does all humanity not know?"

"Because we live in separate and isolated realities."

"This cannot be. It is not Truth."

"No, it isn't. But we humans have the ability and free will to create our own reality; thus, according to our belief, it is fragmented. Humans do not believe in Oneness, thus we do not consciously experience it."

I felt surprise and enormous sympathy. "We share a conscious knowing. As *one* knows, *all* know. Physicality presents challenges and development, but not at the expense of Self-awareness."

"Why do you die on the beaches?" I asked.

"The reasons are physical, but the underlying cause is a movement in consciousness. There are time periods when this happens. Equally, there are long periods when it does not. Physically we resist this, yet we continue to follow the impulses that lead to our beaching. We are consciously linked as we release our bodies, each comforting the others. Our awareness of life always triumphs, for there is no death."

"Humanity believes in death and endings," I said.

I felt from them a genuine empathy of sadness for humanity, and these whales were beached!

"We are aware that humanity has many misconceptions. We have read this in your consciousness as through the ages you have hunted us."

"And you forgive us?"

"Forgiveness has no reality to us, for there is no judgment. Life Is. The conflict in human consciousness is far more of a pain for humanity than the violence you inflict on us. Having now learned of your belief in fragments, your rejection of the Whole, how could you be otherwise?"

How indeed? The Wonder-Neap and I left the whales, staying only until all had died from their bodies. It was a sobering experience. However, when we appeared in another reality, we were now with a single beached whale. This time, several hundred people labored mightily to get one young right whale back into the ocean. Front-end loaders toiled throughout the night to construct a float-way so that the incoming high tide would be accessible to the whale. Teams of people took turns to sit with it, keeping its blanket-covered body saturated as bucket after endless bucket was poured over the whale.

Marine experts were called in, injections of nutrients and antibiotics were given, and everybody who could get near enough to help was there.

The physical action was obvious, but there were other levels in operation. The consciousness of whale and humans was combining, each participating in an empathy that would endure. As the long night passed, the whale withdrew much of its conscious energy, and many people thought it was dying.

The opposite was true. It had made the decision to live, for this encounter had much to offer both species involved. When, with the first pale light of dawn, the tide came in, a keen wind swept hundreds of shivering people as they waded into the cold sea, all eager to help the stranded whale. And they succeeded.

The young right whale now had enough depth to use

its huge flukes and, using the float-way, it slowly made its way out to sea. On the shore, several hundred people laughed, wept, and hugged one another. It was love in action, a triumph in consciousness.

What a change! A few score years earlier, people would have lined up to butcher the whale, carting away the flesh to eat without a thought for it.

Each of the episodes I had experienced in Nature built an overall vision of our present reality as we move into a period of speeded change. Our relationship with the clock remains the same, but Nature and Life do not relate to our measure of time. For consciousness to evolve and expand, life on Earth has no choice but to change. I perceived that our physical life—Nature—is a reflection of consciousness. What we see in the mirror—Nature—is the physical reflection of a much greater metaphysical reality.

I perceived something very challenging. Rather than us being the cause of environmental change, we are the agents. Consciousness is the cause. Our attitude and approach to life is a factor that is speeding things to the point where what once took millions of years is happening in hundreds. I realized that what we see as environmental destruction is a view of life based on separation, on death and endings.

An insight into the evolution of life is neatly depicted by the life of a caterpillar. Is it the ending of life when, inside a chrysalis, a caterpillar goes through a metamorphosis? Titanic forces rip its body apart, yet even as the old body is destructured, a new body is being built. How aptly this describes the life of our times. The action is reciprocal, for consciousness requires a constant physical focus throughout the process. The blueprint of a caterpillar holds a butterfly—a totally different creature. Who knows what the blueprint of an elephant holds? Or of a whale? Or of a toad? Or of a rat? Or of—a human?

In the way that a caterpillar goes through metamorphosis, so our planet, Earth, is going through a similar process. The destructuring we see in Nature and our environment may well herald the demise of many unique expressions of physical form, but it also ushers in the vanguard of new forms of a more mature Nature.

We resist this process for several reasons, but probably the greatest of these is guilt. We know too well our history of violence and natural habitat destruction, and we take on the guilt. My holistic view indicated that we are an intrinsic and vital part of this change, despite our interwoven tangle of emotions, guilt, and attachment to the way things are. Understandably, we blame ourselves.

"Humans need to honor Nature, not feel guilt; you need Self-acceptance in the scheme of life, not self-denial."

"Yes! Humans need many things right now, but if we could only expand our perspective to embrace Wholeness, and let go of the arrogance that lets us think we are in control of life and its destiny, that would help." I sighed deeply. All I could do was share my experience of truth. Like a seed, it would grow in a fertile consciousness, and it, too, would bloom.

❋

With these thoughts, everything changed. I stood in the

Temple of Learning, the Wonder-Neap hovering close by.

"Thank you," I said simply. "What you have shown me will flower in the One human consciousness. It is time."

The Wonder-Neap came close, touching its soft, flexible globe to my head. Put simply, I felt cocooned in love—both from it and for it.

Then it vanished.

9
The Human Nexus

Limitless, endless, unconfined;
that is our truth and the way to live.
Become comfortable with no beliefs,
limits or attachments,
and you become free.

Even as the Wonder-Neap disappeared, Seine came striding toward me.

"Now *that* was a real education. Would you like to relax and renourish?"

I nodded. In silence, we walked into the large room where the invisible force-field seating awaited.

"Can you understand the seating this time?"

"Hmmmm. I think so." I tried to 'inner-feel' for a seat that I knew must be there, but I could detect nothing. Then I had an idea. I visualized myself relaxing, and instantly, as though they had always been visible, I could see seats. None had a base or touched the floor, but they had their own mobility, able to materialize where and when needed, molding and conforming to the need of the Being involved. Now that I could see them, they glowed very faintly, as though phosphorescent. Even as I perceived them, a recliner was waiting for me, so I relaxed into it. The nourishing wave of revitalization began immediately.

Seine said nothing for quite a while, waiting as I took in a nourishment that I had not realized I needed.

"What an incredible plant Being," I said. "But why didn't you take me? Why the Wonder-Neap?"

For a moment, a wishful look flickered over Seine's features. "The Wonder-Neap has unique abilities. I could have accompanied you, but it would have been a more diluted experience. The Wonder-Neap's ability has to do with an empathy between it and its student. It is able to so completely empathize with the student's ever-changing state of emotions and consciousness that it always precipitates the perfect experience in perfect timing. Always! It also has an almost unrivaled ability to enter other realities." He paused. "You should also know that the Wonder-Neap is not a plant. Not in the sense of Earth plants."

This did not surprise me. "Did you know that I have had repetitive dreams about the Wonder-Neap?"

"Yes. More than anything, this indicated its suitability as your guide and mentor."

"It didn't say much."

"Actually, that is not true. It had to communicate with you in a most basic way by projecting verbal words. Even though this is telepathic, it was the equivalent of you having to scream all you want to say at a pitch that would leave your throat sore and painful. In its own way of communicating, it has a prodigious capacity to relay and receive. Beyond words, much of your insight was precipitated by the Wonder-Neap."

"Oh! I should have realized."

We laughed and relaxed, while I relayed much of what

had taken place. I am fairly certain that Seine knew, but he always got me to talk about it. As I talked, the membrane slid slowly across his round, moon eyes. He looked thoughtful for a while, then grew slit-eyed serious. A flutter of alarm awoke in me, but he said nothing until I had finished.

"You have had an overview of the evolving consciousness of animals that will change your relationship with Nature. Now I want you to experience the development of human consciousness — on all levels simultaneously."

"That would be just great," I said brightly, "if I had the faintest idea of what you are suggesting."

"To tell you would be meaningless. It has to be experienced. Trust me."

"Oh, oh! So this is where vulnerable and defenseless come in. Please, Seine, tell me now. How will I experience this? Will I be a participant? Will I know what I know now? Can I get hurt — *really* hurt?"

The enigmatic smile of the sphinx returned. "No, not *really*, but that will be little comfort at the time. You will fully participate, but your reality will expand and change. You will move in and out of a number of identities. Rather than being locked in each time, you will have an ever growing overview, but this overview will not change situations. The people and events are a reality, and you cannot change them. This experience will involve the basest and most violent aspects of humanity, for this is part of its working out. You will —"

"Just hang on a moment," I interrupted. "Base? As in sexual? And violent? As in war?"

Seine shrugged. "It is up to you to determine what the terms mean. After all, it will be your experience."

"Not the way things are going!"

Looking unconcerned, Seine continued. "I was about to say you will also witness a truth, for from the base and violent there emerge love and peace. Do not judge the people concerned, for they are each seeking their own salvation. You may experience the pain of violence—but only briefly. The purpose of the exercise is to experience life at a human level, yet at the same time to perceive the many other levels of Being that are involved. To be frank, you may be hurt, shocked, or become emotionally involved, for you cannot deny your humanity; but you will expand in consciousness, and you will return to your own reality intact."

"I can't wait! In other words, I am not going to see a movie; I am going to star in it. And just to make it more interesting, I am going to be *all* the actors. Right?"

Seine looked surprised. "That sums it up very well. Just a point or two: The actors are *real* players, and don't get attached to happy endings! So, are you willing?"

Reluctantly, I answered, "Yes. I'll do it."

For a brief moment, it seemed that all of reality condensed and expanded simultaneously. I felt a painless inner explosion.

❋

I was walking down a cobbled street in London. My name was Alwyn, and I was in my late twenties. My exact birth date was a mystery, for my parents were dead. Fever killed thousands the year they died, but, of course, they were old, in their forties. I felt a nerve twitching in my back as I strolled along. Joseph was out to get me, and there was no telling when or where that deranged sod might strike. He reckoned that I had seduced his wife, but the truth was that she would bed a man at the drop of a hat. I even told him, but it only made him madder.

Reaching my house, wedged in with others in a dreary row of terraced squalor, I opened the door and went in.

Oh Christ, I thought, trouble.

"Allo, Alwyn. I thought you'd be pleased to see me."

Annie was waiting for me, and it was obvious what she wanted. To make matters more difficult, she was very pretty in a rough, unkempt sort of way.

"Christ, Annie! Joe'll kill me."

"He'll never know, luv. Come on, he gives me a real hard time. So do the others. You're the only gentle one among 'em all. Be kind to yer little Annie."

Christ, but she had an appetite for sex. And she was good at it! Even as I hesitated, she had her hands in the front of my trousers, making things harder than ever. This is the last time, I promised myself yet again, and then I was lost. When it came to sheer lust, Annie took control.

Thirty minutes later, I lay sweating and exhausted. If anything, Annie was just getting started. I groaned in genuine pain as her nails and teeth dug into me, but when the door suddenly flew open, and Joseph strode in, I groaned in a whole different way.

"Joe, it's not what it seems," I squawked.

For a moment I thought it was all right. He smiled at me. "I've been waiting, Alwyn. I've been waiting."

Then, from behind his back, he produced a wicked, long-bladed knife. He didn't hesitate. The first swing caught poor Annie a full smack between her white breasts. And suddenly they were red. The shock on her face held for long moments, then she want slack, as though switched off.

She fell forward onto me as I tried to struggle out from beneath her. Just as I got to my elbows, I felt a heavy blow to the side of my neck. I fell back, paralyzed.

I watched in pain and horror as Joe rolled Annie off me; then, grabbing my flaccid penis, he slashed at it with the knife. Pain exploded in a rolling ball of agony, running up my spine until it burst into my head in a blinding haze of light.

❇

I was standing by the bed, watching Joseph as he stood gaping at the two dead bodies. It was as though he had no idea what he had done.

"Annie! Alwyn! Come on, then. Don't you be tricking me! AAAANNIIEEEEEEEE!"

Annie and I exchanged glances, then stared at our bloody and mutilated bodies. "Oh Christ," I said. "We're dead."

"We can't be," Annie said in a soft, bewildered voice. "I still feel horny."

❇

I whistled as I walked along a cobbled street. My name was Allen, and I was celebrating my eighteenth birthday. I was a bit of a loner, for the locals reckoned that I was weird. My girlfriend and I were about to get married, and I had the strongest impression that I had known her in another life. Harriet was a highly charged girl, so getting married was our priority. If she got in the family way before we were married, there would be hell to pay.

Her bossy mother opposed the marriage, while her dad could not care less. He had little time for Harriet. But her brother was the real problem. He seemed to have a love-hate relationship with both of us. Harry was older than we were, and moody. Harriet was afraid of him. When she was a girl, he would often get into her bed, doing things to her that he should not do. The fact that she liked it only confused her, deepening her guilt while inciting a deep resentment of him.

That was the way things stood, and in a week Harriet and I were going to have a quiet wedding with only a few people invited. I only had my dad alive, and he would do anything for a quiet life.

I was on my way to Harriet's place. As I reached the terraced house, I could hear some people arguing. I knocked and went in. Harry was standing flushed and angry, while Harriet was beside herself with rage. I stared at them, and flashes of another vision flickered into my mind. I saw a bed with Harriet—no, Annie—sprawled naked over me—no, I was Alwyn. Harry stood over us with a knife—no, he was Joseph. But who were these people that seemed to have our persona?

190

As my vision returned to normal, with surging anger I noticed that Harriet's clothing was in disarray.

I glared at Harry, "You despicable bastard," I snarled.

"It was her. She's a slut," he cried.

"You bloody liar," Harriet screamed. "You can't bear Allen and I having sex. You think you can still force me the way you did when we were kids."

Lost in rage, I grabbed at the kitchen drawer where all the cutlery was kept, my hand closing over a knife. I drew it out—seeing Joseph swing the blade into Annie's chest—and I threw it at him as hard as I could.

What a fluke! The knife slammed into Harry over his heart, and he was dead before he hit the floor. Harriet and I gaped in horror. We were frozen in shock.

"Oh God! Now what?" I asked.

❄

I walked briskly down the street. London had had streetlights recently installed, and the gaslight made it safer for all concerned. I had a focus in my identity of Leonard, but I was aware of being more than Leonard. I also had a focus in a young lady, a singer known as Amber, and, as if that were not enough, I had a focus in a man named Mark. He was Amber's lover and a very envied man. Amber was a beauty. Unknown to Mark, Leonard was also Amber's lover, for along with her beauty went a fair appetite for healthy sex.

In an odd sort of way, I was each individually, yet I was all three simultaneously. But there was more. I was aware

191

of shadow selves. These shadow selves were formed from the thoughts and desires of the people they shadowed. They seemed to take on an abstract form duplicating their person; they were a shadow in the human psyche.

I learned that they could influence their human self. Leonard's shadow self whispered into his head, becoming his own thoughts. It talked to him almost nonstop, filling his waking hours with jealous thoughts—negative thoughts that devalued him.

So it was also with Mark and Amber. Their thoughts were very similar—sex! As much as possible, in every way possible, whenever possible. Very uncomplicated. Their shadow selves echoed their desires, shaping new ideas of lust and gratification in which they could engage. But there was something else. Beneath the overwhelming sexuality was love. Amber and Mark had never even discussed love—sex was enough—but in the depths of their hearts love was stirring, becoming empowered.

As Leonard, I had recently found out about Mark. It had been a shock to discover that I shared Amber's body with him. I had known Mark for ages, but I had never dreamt that he was fornicating with my woman. However, it would soon end. For the last few weeks, I had been plotting to kill Mark. I intended to have the lovely lady for myself. My plan was very simple. I had invited Amber and Mark around for dinner this very evening. Unbeknown to them, one of the after-dinner drinks would contain a slow poison, and this would be Mark's. Amber and Mark would be long gone when he died. I felt a genuine regret about this. I rather liked Mark. I would even have preferred to chal-

lenge him honorably to a private duel, but he would almost
certainly have won. I had no intentions of getting killed
over the lady.

I reached my fine house, and on entering I called my
butler, detailing the final arrangements for the evening dinner. Everything would be perfectly attended to, and I intended to spare no expense. Mark would die, but at least
he would be honorably wined and dined!

As Mark, I viewed the evening with keen anticipation.
Leonard was known to be an excellent dinner host, and
his reputation was legend for fine after-dinner drinks.

I collected Amber in the buggy, and the driver took us
the long way around the park. We had privacy in the buggy,
and it was not long before Amber had my passions in-
flamed. Her sharp little teeth dug into my neck, and her
sharp nails dug through the satin of my breeches. I looked
and felt indecent, but my blood rushed giddily through my
veins. I'm not quite sure how we managed it, with all her
layers of petticoats and skirts, but Amber found a way. She
pulled, pushed, grabbed, and squirmed, and when it happened I was a hot poker in a flaming fire.

As Amber, I relaxed with a flushed sigh. I had an intensity of energy that could find only one satisfaction, but I was
aware of a change. I knew now that I loved Mark. Sex
was no longer enough, I wanted his baby, even despite my
career as a singer. Tonight, before we left, I would discreetly tell Leonard that it was finished between us.

They came together—Leonard, Mark, and Amber—
and the evening was a fine success. Each was successful
in his or her own particular field of endeavor, and each

had plenty to contribute to the diverse and interesting conversation.

The shadow selves, each in their own psyche, spoke of different things. The thoughts of Leonard strayed constantly to the glass that held a single drop of a rare but very efficient poison. He felt increasing sympathy for Mark, wishing there could be some other way. Amber had quite different thoughts. Her shadow self suggested over and over that she could not trust Leonard. Try as she might, she could not dismiss thoughts of danger.

Mark was having new thoughts. He noticed the obvious familiarity between Leonard and Amber, and he wondered if her passions and beautiful body had ever wrapped around Leonard.

And so the meal progressed.

After dinner, they all adjourned to the lounge, while servants cleaned away the meal and brought in the drinks.

"Try this—you'll enjoy this one," Leonard said, as he poured them each a glass of an amber fluid. The glasses had just been handed out when a loud crash followed by a scream came from the kitchen.

With a quiet oath, Leonard placed his drink on a small table and walked briskly out of the room.

Following an impulse, Amber walked over to Mark, picked up his glass, and held it to the light. "Hmmm, thought I saw a crack in it." Pretending to need better light, she walked past the small table and, unseen by Mark, switched glasses. "No, I must have imagined it," she said, as she handed the drink back to him. She kissed him, her hands lingering in provocative places.

When Leonard came in, they were sitting discreetly apart, sipping the fine old whiskey.

"Damn cook. Stupid woman. A lot of fuss about nothing. Enjoying the whiskey?"

"Excellent. Absolutely first-class," Mark said with enthusiasm.

Later, when Mark excused himself from the room, Amber took her opportunity.

"I won't beat around the bush, Leonard," she said, setting his heart racing in a flutter of fear, "but it is all over between us. Mark and I are getting married."

Her own comment surprised her, but she knew that it would come to pass. After all, she thought, smiling secretly, in her hands Mark was willing for anything. She was also surprised at how gracefully Leonard accepted it.

"Well, if ever you should need me, I am always at your service," he said with unsubtle innuendo.

The evening came to a close. With many overly gushing farewells, Mark and Amber climbed once more into the buggy and headed to Amber's home. Apart from sexual overtures, they made it without incident, for they both had other things on their minds. Somewhat to his surprise, Mark found that he was frightened of losing Amber to Leonard.

His question caught him as much by surprise as Amber. "I say, Amber, will you marry me?"

"Oh, Mark. Yes. Yes. Yes. I want your baby . . . now!"

As the three in one, yet individually as each of the three, I went as Mark and Amber up to Amber's bedroom and got heavily involved in baby making. It was fun.

As Leonard, I also went to bed. By the time I discovered that it was I, not Mark, who was dying, it was far too late to prevent it. But I did have time to laugh and to realize with some surprise that I felt no anger or malice toward them at all.

My focus combined with all three of them, and the conflict was resolved. The long interplay among the oversexed Annie/Harriet/Amber and her lovers, Alwyn/Allen/Mark and Joseph/Harry/Leonard, had come to an end. Three lifetimes had been devoted to resolving their lust, hate, and violence. Amber had found that her overpowering sexuality had always contained a core of love, but it had taken her a long time to find it. Mark had enjoyed illicit relationships, flirting on the edge of danger, but he, too, had responded to love. Leonard, however, had taken a great leap in consciousness, resolving the deadlock by accepting his death and releasing all attachments to the woman. He had also found love—a love that encompassed them all. As he died, he wished them well. He was also very glad that his compassion had prompted him to choose an expensive but quite painless poison!

I was the nexus among these three people. I knew that they were a microcosm of the vast, complex macrocosm of humanity. I had learned also of shadow selves. Just as their shadow selves were born from the mental energy and focus they created, so it is with all humanity. I also witnessed their shadow selves grow several degrees lighter as they found the love to resolve their long continuity of conflict.

❋

Everything changed. As Self, I became aware of a vast hologram in which countless people acted out the drama of their lives. I perceived all this from an overview, my perspective gradually moving closer. I had no shape or form; I was a watcher. As I got closer, I perceived countless holograms all individually projected by the people within the One vast overall hologram. I became part of a small crowd of people walking down the street in modern London toward an underground station. I was every person in that crowd, yet I was also the crowd as a whole. As each person, I was in a crowd of strangers, but from the greater perspective of the consciousness of the crowd, I knew that every person had links with the others that went back many lifetimes.

I was Betty, worrying about my sick father, and I was Fred, cheating on my wife as I hurried to meet another woman. I was Bert, drunk, and struggling with an alcoholic problem. I was Ivy, coping with the fear of just losing her job as a secretary. I was Jane, a glamorous stripper and call girl, stunned by the news of breast cancer and hating my overgenerous breasts. I was Mathew, playing hooky from school. I was a child in a pram, seeing life with a simplicity and clarity that adults, in their complexity, lose. I was Reggie, on my way to the outpatient's clinic, and I was Carol, late, and hurrying for a date.

I was also Patricia, with a primed bomb in the innocent pram I had left just inside the crowded station. I was all these people and more, as each projected his or her personal hologram of hope or despair, of love or hate, positive or negative. And beyond it all, somehow containing it, a vast hologram of the collective beliefs of humanity added its influence to the masses of personal holograms. Only I witnessed the shadow selves, each one part of the human who created it. Some shone with a luminosity, for the focus of their selves was uplifting, while others wore a deep gloom that penetrated the physical counterpart. In some of these people, malignant growths were beginning, precipitated by their own constant thoughts of self-deprecation. But in that hurrying crowd, shadow selves were unknown, disregarded. Only I witnessed the other layers of reality that seemed to be another picture projected onto the same screen, yet a picture that held a perfect juxtaposition to the drama of the small crowd. In each personal hologram, the shadow selves merged unnoticed. Unnoticed also were selves of the past and selves of the future, all contributing to the makeup of the shadow selves and dovetailing their realities to fit perfectly with the unsuspecting present self of the eternal Now.

The bomb ticked silently. All the shadow selves knew of it, for their mental energy could penetrate personal barriers, and Patricia, her heart hammering as she stood across the street waiting, was broadcasting her apprehension on a very powerful wave of fear. Despite her anxiety, she had no idea of the awful power of the bomb that was primed and waiting.

The blast was a sudden angry roar of violence and carnage. Although prepared, a shocked Patricia immediately rushed across the street to see what had happened. As she raced into the debris, she tripped over an upturned pram, rolling onto the headless body of a child. She shrieked, scrambling to her feet, but again she tumbled, her foot turning on a small, pulped head that stared at her with the open eyes of innocence. She vomited. She would be haunted by the nightmare of that face for the rest of her life. A sucker for a cause, she realized too late that she had been duped by the fanatics who had conned her into believing that the bomb would produce no more than a lot of smoke and noise.

Fred sat in a pile of rubble, crying softly as his entrails coiled in a slow, sinister cluster over his knees. He felt no pain, but as his life ebbed swiftly away, he was filled with the most profound regret. Jane was silent, her hated breasts a bloody mess; she had died instantly. Betty would never reach her sick father, yet in life's perfect synchronism, he suffered a massive heart attack in the moment the bomb exploded. Poor Reggie, who haunted the outpatients' clinic more for company than for any real problem, would now have many years of compulsory visits. A strip of metal from the pram had transfixed his head, going in the right ear and piercing out through his left cheek. He groaned in a loud monotone of pain and stark fear. Bert had been in an alcoholic stupor as he ambled into the underground. The blast had thrown him, limp as a rag doll, into the street. Now, shock sobered and minus most of his clothing, he was already helping the injured. In a long life that was to be committed to the service of humanity, he would never again drink alcohol. Poor Ivy lost not only her job but her life. Mathew would never play hooky from school again, but he lived. He would need to learn special skills, for he was permanently blinded. And Carol was very late for her date — about three months and half a leg late — but he loved her, and he waited.

All this and more unfolded, for this was only a small part of the crowd — a representation. Where people died, shadow selves faded quickly, vanishing but not finished. They were not good or bad, these shadow selves; they were a hidden, unrealized reflection of the persona. As the people were compelled by death to vacate their bodies, so recognition spread among them. Beings of Light were there, and although I did not see the Lady Gold, there were many like her. The people who believed in death as the End were gently ushered into an area of powerful, ethereal Light, while other, more open souls were being attended to by the Light Beings.

On a physical level, there was chaos and carnage, fear, pain, and suffering. On a soul level, there were quick groupings taking place as some realized that death was a transition. While they had been rubbing shoulders with strangers, when physical, now they knew better; they were among friends. It was almost as though this was a long-planned and carefully organized exodus.

And, of course, it was. From an overview perspective, I could see the formation of this accident/purpose in the making. Each person involved had organized his or her life so as to be in this exact place at this exact time. In each personal hologram, a linking had taken place, each with the others, all dovetailing with their destinies in the One overall human hologram. For some, it was a form of self-punishment, a gleaning of the past that, denying self-forgiveness, was seeking retribution. A few held a desire to die, believing death to be the end of all their problems. They were in for a shock! The child was aware that it had already expressed its purpose in this lifetime, and it was keen to get on with the next. It knew that with a few more years of adult influence all its clarity of inner knowing would be smothered and lost. Only the child was an aware participant. An old soul at six months, it knew that it was soul-bonded to Vera, its mother, so naturally enough they were together when the explosion killed them.

Instead of a child soul releasing the baby's body, a vibrant, ageless, youthful woman helped the dazed man who was released from Vera's body. "That was a shock," the man said, "even though on a soul level we planned to be in this together." They stood for long moments, soul-bonded, radiant in Light and knowing, before they began to assist the lost people who had not developed their awareness of the continuity of life. But even as they separated, their soul-bond remained; a bond forever connecting them across time, space, and realities.

I witnessed all of this and more. Two of the people who died in the explosion were on their way to meet at their lawyer's. Skip and Donna were about to get a divorce after years of bitter wrangling. Each had left the other many times, but always something drew them back, some inexplicable thread of affection or caring they did not understand.

Now, they were both in the group that rapidly and easily assimilated their death and transition. They found they were drawn to each other as though irresistible magnets. I was both of them individually, as a pair, and as an observer. As an observer, I witnessed the soul-bond that linked them—a bond that went beyond personality problems, sexes, age, relationship to each other, even death.

As Skip, I experienced a surge of insight and clarity as I watched a shining woman arise from the horrific and shattered body of a headless child. It rekindled a knowing so deep and powerful that I was shocked that I could ever lose it. But I had. In this incarnation, I had forgotten so much. In my newfound knowing, I realized that I had planned to be part of this exodus into Light with my soul-bonded Donna.

As Donna, I was lost, dazed, bewildered. I was staring at a man I recognized as Skip, yet he was more than Skip, for he was Dougal and Hugh and other identities I remembered in a long succession of lives we had shared. I remembered being his mother, and later his son. Once, he had been a woman—my secret mistress—and, oh God! . . . I had killed her, but always the connection between us had persisted. He walked over to me, and amid all the shadowy destruction of a bomb blast, we kissed, our lips, our hearts, and our souls meeting in a blaze of Light. From this moment on, I knew my focus would always be on the highest ideals that I could express—my Self.

Leaving Donna, and all other identities, my overview widened and deepened, and my perception revealed more. In some way, this incident linked with the dramatic and violent evolution of Nature. But I could see the basic difference: Nature's evolution was a response to environmental changes coupled with the pressure to physically survive. Human development came from a reaction to emotional and mental pressures coupled with the focus of the soul. Each created an arena of conflict — a natural dynamic — and from this came many levels of growth. Nature's pressures were external and humanity's were internal, yet each were intertwined and interlinked in the Oneness of Life. The forces of destructuring that gave birth to a butterfly were the same forces that propelled and compelled all humanity through the trauma of change to find our greatest potential.

☀

Change and expansion gripped me. All sense of human physicality fell away, while my sense of Self expanded. I was now part of the mass human psyche, aware of individual people, yet in consciousness I encompassed all people. I was able to view humanity on planet Earth as a Whole, perceiving all places and people at one and the same moment. My perception embraced the Whole, but my focus remained with the group of people in the bomb blasted underground railway station of a busy street in London.

I watched the interplay and juxtaposition of reality. Betty's body was being placed on a stretcher, seemingly unmarked, yet pulped beneath her clothing. Her father, who had simultaneously died from a massive heart attack, hovered nearby, remarkably alert and aware. I saw that he was encased in a nonphysical universe/reality — an entire universe of his own. He was unknowingly influencing his universe to encompass Betty, and he was succeeding. As his metaphysical Self embraced Betty, turning her away from the attachment to her grief, she realized that her beloved father was with her. I perceived that these, too, were a soul-bonded pair.

But it was the multiple metaphysical universes that held my attention. From an even greater perspective, I could now see that every person in the purpose/accident lived in his or her own universe—as indeed, did *every* human Being. Each universe was programmed by its unwitting tenant with a design to manifest his or her beliefs and focus in life.

I watched Fred, one of the believers in death, lost in his limbo universe of gray shadows, yet it occupied the same space and time as the Light universe of Skip and Donna. His limited belief had created a different reality.

I saw, by being a player—all the players—that we each create our own reality. We each live in a metaphysical universe that responds to our own program. It responds, never judges. If our mental program is uplifting, our universe responds; if our program is a killer, it also responds. In all their simultaneous, multilevels of reality, each of the people followed his or her own beliefs and conditioning, while the universe/reality shaped itself accordingly.

Jane wallowed in self-disgust for the way she had lived. With her lush figure, stripping and prostitution had been a sure way to make money during hard times, yet this had fostered a self-hatred that was now expressed in a universe of sulphurous cloud and anger. Yet all those who had died in the crowd had chosen to die together. Ivy quickly overcame the illusions of death; releasing her dead body, she stared at the shocked metaphysical aspect of Jane.

"Sister May!" she called. "Don't you remember me?"

Jane stared in apathy. "Who?"

"I remember you. We were in a convent together in a life before this. You were there because of your denial of your sexuality. You hated men. I remember how we used to argue about you running away from the issue of sex."

"But . . . I'm a stripper . . . and a prostitute."

"Were, Sister May, were. Nun and stripper—it's all in the past. This is a new beginning."

But Jane was incapable of comprehension. Ivy went over to her; putting her arms around Jane, she imagined Light surrounding them both, and she embraced her with love. It happened. I watched Jane release her guilt-laden reality of self-loathing, allowing Ivy's love to reprogram her own universe and become her new reality creation.

※

Gradually, all that was happening moved beyond explanation or description. I expanded and contracted simultaneously, becoming the part and the All, knowing they were One. Gradually, I became aware of a presence of vast consciousness, a multidimensional Intelligence far beyond my comprehension.

※

I was standing in a chamber of astronomical proportions.

I perceived that the chamber *was* the Being of Intelligence, or part of it. Everything was on a prodigious, yet ethereal scale.

"Summarize your experience. Let it filter through your thoughts, your perception, your awareness, your intuition, your consciousness. With all that you are, recapitulate the essence of your experience. Let it flow, and I will clarify and guide you."

I was filled and expanded by the power of the communication. I focused on all that had taken place, and everything abruptly changed.

The vast, planet-sized chamber was now an immense hologram, and in this mammoth projection all humanity was acting out their individual roles as though cast in some never-ending cosmic play. As I watched the limitless Intelligence, It and I became more fused in awareness, and my sense of Self expanded beyond all ability to describe. I saw the play being enacted in all time and in all places at one and the same moment.

The past, present, and future were one movement in one coordinated happening, a self-determined orchestration that was balanced and counterbalanced with the birth of each action projected by a player. Not only was a physical humanity living its act in this incredible hologram, but the dimension of thought also wove its messages of deceit and truth in the form of personal shadow selves interplaying with all of the physical selves. As though this were not enough, the incarnated identities that each person had lived, both past and future, were all part of the human movement as each individual tried to find the truth of Self.

Each shadow self reflected the thoughts of the thinker in either degrees of light or intensity of shadow. All of this I encompassed into awareness with astonishing ease. There was no longer "my" awareness, only *awareness*.

I was both the watcher of the players and part of the psyche of all the players in the hologram. In this way, I became the experience. Gradually, the hologram encompassed not only the people of Earth, but also the entire universe.

Within this vast, all-encompassing awareness, where I still retained awareness of my individuality within the One (individuality, not identity), I felt a shock of surprise. I perceived, experienced, realized that our universe as a Whole—which is a sentient Being—has as many aspects of individuality as a human Being. I perceived that in the One physical space of planet Earth, there are as many realities of Earth as there are pairs of soul-bonded human Beings.

As, in my perception, I became One with All Life on Earth, I realized that each and every human Being truly does create his or her own reality. We each live in our own world. We each choose—and not choosing is also a choice—exactly how we will experience our world, even what we will have in it. And the choice or lack of choice is made every time we respond or react to a person or situation. With our imagination, emotions, thoughts, actions, reactions, and responses, we are creating our own universe/reality every moment of our lives.

To protect ourselves from the mass insanity of experiencing ourselves as the only person, or the only soul-bonded pair, in our universe, we each project an impression of a universe that is the same as everybody else's projection of the universe—consensus reality. In other words, we project a mass hallucination that we all believe in and call the "real" universe. It is no more than an elaborate illusion!

I perceived the Principle of Truth. Each and every person's universe is programmed to support his or her personal beliefs and focus. As I watched from a perspective of involvement, I knew that our focus and beliefs are based on the falsity, half-truths, and lies of fear and separation. I experienced each and every person as a Being of Light. A focus on this Truth creates more Light, while a focus away from this creates more shadow. Not for a moment did the Light ever get less, but the illusions of shadow made it appear less.

Within this multidimensional hologram, I encompassed a greater knowing of the soul-bonded pairs of humans. Sometimes these pairs may be married; other times they may be enemies. Sometimes they may be poles apart on the planet; at other times, next-door neighbors. Sometimes related, sometimes friends, sometimes lovers, sometimes unknown to each other. They may be opposite sexes or the same sex. But above and beyond the personal, identity-based relationships, these soul-bonded pairs reflect a Oneness of Self that will never allow the illusion of separation to become absolute. The urge for each member of a soul-bonded pair is to find his or her "other half," for this creates a greater sense of Wholeness and Love. There are occasions, however, when a person knows intuitively that the other half of his or her soul-bond has not incarnated at this time. Being alone allows a different, but equally creative, expression of Self. Each soul-bonded pair tends to follow its continuity of life on a course that is constantly familiar.

As I witnessed this vast, all-encompassing holographic projection, I perceived that each person is both the projector and a player in a hologram of his or her own making. In this way, we protect our sanity by creating an illusion we all relate to. The paradox that I witnessed is that while we each project a uniform hologram to protect us from the despair of isolation, the illusion we have projected has manifested itself in the self-deceit of separation. It would appear that this is self-defeating, but there is more.

Within the vast hologram, I perceived change moving into the individual hologram/personal universe of each pair of soul-bonded humans. Not a quiet and gentle expression of change, but a powerful volcanic force that is about to hit humanity with all the concern of a tornado for a forest. But again, the paradox, for this is changeless change. Within the vast hologram—the essence of every personal hologram—is only Oneness. Not one individual is separate, nor is it possible to be. No matter how much people react from fear, each person's reaction is instantly counterbalanced. Not even this fear-based reaction is excluded from the actions of the Whole. Within the Whole—which is Truth expressing Self—nothing changes, yet, paradoxically, all is constant, dynamic change. Change and changelessness are One, the eternal dynamic balance and counterbalance of the movement in the moment.

All this became my reality, far more than words or even thoughts can describe. All this became my experience, my wholeness, my beingness, my totality. To encompass the sheer magnitude of experience, of necessity my intellect became still and silent, while that which I am—Self— expanded and stretched. I became aware of Self as vast, reaching out to embrace the furthermost reaches of the Beyond, while, simultaneously, I was the most minute mote in a particle of cosmic dust.

※

After an endless time of no time, beyond and betwixt exhilaration and exhaustion, I rested in some eternal dimension of Silence.

10
Universal Matrix

As the sap rises and falls within a tree,
and in the manner that blood is vital to all animals,
so the spiritual Intelligence of Self
is a dance of Light within our Beings.

As I came out of my period of rest, I was standing on the surface of a strange planet. I knew that I was with the Being who had empowered my recent experience, but even after the habitat of the Being of Beauty, this was a bizarre and startling reality.

I stood in front of what appeared to be a Brain of the most colossal proportions. This was not *a* brain, it was *the* Brain, with an omnipotence that was very careful not to overpower me. The Brain seemed to grow from the earth in the way a tree would grow, except that the Brain may well have covered a hundred acres. Vision was not limited to my eyes, for my light-body Self had a sense of perception that was all-embracing. Distance was not really distance at all, for sight was as clear a hundred acres away as it was in my immediate vicinity; yet, paradoxically, distance remained, creating a sense of proportion and perspective.

I would have expected to feel revulsion at the sight of a naked Brain; instead, I felt an awe and reverence that was religious in its intensity. I looked around for the vastly different and much more graceful needle spires of the Temple of Learning, but they were not to be seen.

The Brain was growing from what appeared to be an endless desert. There was no vegetation at all, while the sand was a pale rose pink, similar in color to the Brain, which was several shades darker. I bent over and scooped a handful, allowing it to trickle through my fingers. It was alive! How this was possible I could not even surmise, but I felt its aliveness. Even more than that, I felt its awareness.

"This is not Earth, nor does it have any physical reality. You are with the Brain of Planetary Awareness."

I gasped. "What's that?"

"I am not a what, nor am I a thing. Neither am I a place, nor can I be conceptualized. I am Awareness. No more, no less. Nothing I can say relates to the intellect, because there is no intellectual reference to me. Awareness Is."

"But that doesn't make sense."

"Not to you. How can you intellectually understand a reality that is not intellectually possible? How can I explain that which has no explanation. I am real. Do you accept that?"

The words seemed to fade away, and I was trying to grasp the implications when I felt a mist descending over me. I struggled to avoid it, dodging to one side, but it was as useless as trying to avoid water while swimming in a river. Everything blurred and hazed around me, and I felt that I was being swept into the air and hurtled along at tremendous speed. Gradually, the mist cleared and I no longer felt movement. As the last traces rapidly vanished, I found that I was inside an immense planet-sized chamber.

I *knew,* without a shred of doubt, that I was inside the Brain. I gulped, yet it was not fear I experienced. This was the place of holograms, where my human nexus had taken place. I knew also that it had deliberately revealed this aspect of its reality to me. Even as I knew that I was inside the Brain, I knew that there was no outside. The whole planet was Brain. Outside or inside had no defined reality.

Everywhere was lit up far brighter than on a sunny day on Earth—an illumination coming from an inner unseen source. Looking around the huge cavern, I noticed that the floor was the same rose pink sand, while the walls—if they could be so named—were undoubtedly Brain. My knowing also revealed that the Brain communicated directly into my awareness, expanding it. "To the degree you are able, experience the purpose of the Self of Life," it told me.

❋

Thinking and definitions came to an end. Within the dichotomy of a vast, filled emptiness I lived and play-died in the essence of spirit and form. Awareness expanded and experienced—Brain and I as One—yet my individuality persisted. Brain opened up the All That Is to the degree of my ability to encompass the infinite Isness of spiritual expression.

❋

Let me tell this in the only way I can humanly find to tell of something that defies telling.

214

In the beginning, there is no beginning, for beginnings and endings are time and intellect related. Beingness Is!

Isness is Divine Principle—God, God Self, Self, Love, Pure Light, the I Am, the Force—call it what you will. Each human Being is an expression and an aspect of this Divine Principle. To express my Self of the Divine Principle, I utilize my creative power to manifest consciousness. Once manifest, consciousness is aware of Self as Divine Principle, and I spin out threads of conscious awareness, seeding an infinite number of possible expressions through an infinite number of dimensions and realities. Physical and metaphysical, ethereal and corporeal, plus infinite endless states of Being that have neither human meaning or definition, All is One. All this is the expression of Divine Principle. Divine Principle is Truth, and with Truth goes purpose. My purpose is that the One shall experience infinite variations and definitions of individuality, all with the purpose of the individual realizing Self as the One—the All That Is.

As consciousness, manifest by my own Divine Principle, I am designed to create, so I draw substance into Being. I also create other variations of nonphysical reality. However, I will describe the creative process only as it pertains to us, for this is also *your* story and *your* reality.

Using Light as a vehicle and tool, for an eternity of Isness (time), I consciously express Self in a huge variety of gas life, all nonphysical and volatile. I am nameless, formless, and without substance. I occupy a state we will call space, yet this also is the All That Is. For a huge span of Isness, I seek to extend every potential. I am gaseous, sometimes volatile, sometimes inert. I expand, and I contract. I freeze, and I boil. In countless different ways, I form and explore new gases. I am liquid fire. I am liquid water. I am solid. I melt. I evaporate. I am heavy. I am light. But always I have a purpose. I seek to know Self as individual within the One. But I do not find Self as individual; I am One, and All gas is One gas.

In my creative process of Self-expression, I mold and manipulate the vibrations of Light, and I become dense physical matter. I am gas, and I am mineral life. I become planet Earth. Over an indeterminate period—in a mind-boggling linear time construct—I explore both gas and minerals together, for I always retain that which I am. I experience the solidifying of gas in many millions of variations, forming a vast digression of mineral forms, yet always I am Self as One. My mineral form experiences no individuality in its many different expressions, only a diversity of One. Following the developing Earth, my evolving consciousness seeks a higher expression of awareness in this one particular creation among infinite other creations of the Divine Principle.

I am gas, mineral, and, now, plant life. As my evolving consciousness expands, I draw to Self a new form through which to explore variable individuality. My beginnings are primitive. I am algae living in water; I am lichens corroding rock. I am mosses extending potential, and I grow. I am ferns. I am palms. I am grasses. I am the flowers that express continuity, and I am the great trees. I cover the planet Earth, and I fertilize it. I develop and grow over enormous spans of time, and I develop and explore the miracle of pollination, so that I may continue this expression of Self. But always Self is One. Despite the complex and diverse multitude of life, all Nature knows Self as One. There is no individuality.

Once again, containing the consciousness of gas, mineral, and plant life, I continue my expansion and search for creative expressions of individuality. While exploring the plant experience, I simultaneously follow the natural extrapolation of animal life.

I am tiny amoeba, single celled, simple. I am huge dinosaur, many celled, simple. I abound in a multitude of insects. I explore in an ever-changing pattern of more and more complex animal forms. I am herbivorous. I am omnivorous. I am carnivorous. I am hare. I am bear. I am lion. I am a huge, cold-blooded reptile fighting for supremacy on the water's edge. I am a tiny possum lapping nectar from a flower. I am a flock of birds wheeling in the sky, each twist and turn a perfect orchestration of attunement. I am a herd of wildebeest racing across the plains, plunging to death in a raging river as I run blindly with the herd.

I am gas, mineral, plant, and animal life—I contain each and all. I am the consciousness beyond form. I seek always to find Self in the individual expression of One. Where there is a cell in a leaf, the blueprint of the whole plant is held within the cell. Nature cannot separate Divine Principle. In the gas, mineral, and plant kingdoms, there is no expression of the individuality that I seek. All gas, minerals, and plants know Self as One. Consciousness reaches as far as the expression of an individual species, but not individuality within the species. However, as I draw to Self the animal kingdom, within which to explore the potential of Self-realization, the beginnings of individuality begin to occur. Certain species give birth to individualistic expression. The most basic and simple expressions of reason are born and developed. But within this frame of Nature, another expression waits its moment of truth—imagination!

I am gas, mineral, plant, animal, and humanity. But I am more. I am not only the evolvement of Nature; I am also a mixing with other threads of creation. As human, I encompass the stars. I encompass other realities, yet, physically, I am Earthbound. I have imagination. I have the potential to fully experience individuality *and* to know Self as One with the Divine Principle. The correct use of imagination is my key to Self-realization.

I am Self expressing through physical form, yet my quest for Self-realization is weak, while my instinct to survive and dominate physically is strong. I am a creator, yet I am without any realization of what this means. Unwittingly, I create that which will enslave me: fear.

My fear becomes the crucible of the supreme lie, creating the illusion that All Life is separate. Lost in this illusion, I experience separation instead of Oneness, identity instead of individuality, conflict instead of cooperation, competition instead of participation, the mundane instead of the magnificent. In separation, the great deceit is born, the illusion that life is an external, physical expression, rather than a spiritual expression of Self.

And, yet, the paradox. It is my humanity, lost in its separation, that has the potential to eventually experience individuality *and* know Self. This is still a potential, because the highest expression of individuality occurs only when the illusion of separation has been shattered. Humanity experiences personality and identity, *not* real individuality. Only the release of identity will allow my expression of individuality to manifest as Self.

I am purpose. My Divine Principle Self gave birth to my purpose by extending Self through the infinite creations of potential Self-realization. I am humanity. My purpose is to release my ego-centered identity and move into that exultant moment of Self-realization.

When, one by one, we recognize Divine Principle, a cycle within a great eternal cycle becomes fulfilled. Within this process—which the mind can witness, but not experience—there is the movement of Spirit. As the sap rises and falls in a tree, and in the manner that blood is vital to all animals, so the Spirit of Self is a dance of Light within our Beings. I feel this movement. I am this movement. I am humanity. I/we feel this in transcendent moments, when we are expressing love, or are being creative, sensitive, and aware.

I am humanity, and I experience my purpose. In the moment I *know* my Self as One with All, my identity no longer has any *real* meaning, and I am individual within the Whole. In this moment, the Self of Divine Principle expands—the All That Is expands—and my purpose is revealed. I am humanity. As my awareness grows to encompass Truth, so Self expands, for in my particular thread of the creation of Divine Principle, I am the substance of its growth. I become the movement of a cycle within a cycle, for as I—the Self of Divine Principle—create movement, so movement creates a greater awareness. And in this cycle, the expansion of awareness keeps the Divine Principle in movement. I am humanity, and I am the Divine Principle expanding conscious awareness by creative action.

※

For what seems as infinity, Silence prevails. I enter the experience of other expressions of the threads of creation from Divine Principle, but only as Awareness. Brain is both the carrier and catalyst of all these connections—a Being of Intelligence and Awareness so far beyond human intellect that I become mute. Only Silence can hold the experience.

Brain is also manifest compassion, for in a way that I cannot comprehend, not for a moment do I feel overwhelmed or the least bit insignificant. Nature taught me a while back that insignificance is another human concept, for in Truth all is One. But to experience infinity within the vast Awareness of Brain and not feel reduced indicates a depth of sensitivity beyond definition.

The experience triggers knowing, some instantly available while other knowing emerges under the prompting of daily living. Moving as a nonphysical projection of Brain's Awareness through the dimensions and realities of the "multiverse" in which we live, I perceive that dark is only a temporal construct of three-dimensional reality. I perceive no dark, no space, no distance, yet it is vast beyond imagination. I experience Light as the illumination of eternity. I experience all humanity as eternal Beings of Light.

At some point in this omnipresent experience, I move into a state of suspension, as though deeply asleep while wide awake. I become aware that my impression of Brain is not its true reality. My way of perceiving it was based on an aspect of its reality that I could accept. On a deep inner level, I am now able to encompass Brain as the pure consciousness of Awareness. Brain is Light. And in this benevolent Light, I float in a cocoon of peace.

※

As though coming out of a pleasant sleep, I became aware once more of standing in the vast, faintly pulsating, chamber of Brain. Even as I wondered what would happen next, once again that mist descended over me, somehow smothering all will and movement. Even as I felt the hurtling speed, I surrendered to it, becoming vulnerable, and all mist and hurtling speed instantly ended. As though in a tunnel of Light, I could see Seine at the far end, and without hurry or anxiety, I strolled toward him. Maybe this was how Seine did it, for I was with him in less than three paces.

I was irrevocably changed by my experience of Oneness. I had almost experienced too much. I felt immeasurably old, ancient beyond time; in some deep inner place, I felt that I had wept an ocean of tears for the plight of humanity.

While Seine and I silently hugged, I looked around for the Brain, but only the needle spires of the Temple of Learning were to be seen. The Brain of Planetary Awareness had vanished. For a moment, a hundred questions invaded my mind, but I released them. It simply did not matter. An intellectual pursuit of something beyond intellectual understanding was the last thing I needed!

Seine smiled his approval. I stared at him. He seemed to be flickering with gold in a way I had never before seen, while his eyes were silver moons of clear knowing.

He pointed to somewhere or something behind him.

"Do you see those Doors?"

I stared where he had indicated, peering around him. "No, I don't. Where are they?"

He smiled. "I did not think you could, although I must admit, you never fail to surprise me."

"All is not known then?" I asked.

"No. A probability pattern is always evident, but humanity really does have free will within the confinements that you unwittingly create."

I thought about the Doors I could not see. I seem to have spent lifetimes finding Doors and struggling to pass through them. Having so recently succeeded, once again I was in the vicinity of other Doors to a further Beyond, and I could not even see them!

"Why can't I see the Doors?"

"Because it is not yet your moment to pass through them. You cannot see and enter these Doors and retain an Earth body."

"Does this mean that on some planet your body has died? I never thought of you as having a physical body."

"I did not have a physical body, as you call it, so I do not have a body that has recently died," Seine replied. "There is a timing to Truth, for life is Truth expressing

Self. While this moment holds both my timing and my Truth, these particular Doors are not yet within your timing."

He looked at me, while I choked up.

"Can't I come?" I pleaded.

"Don't get attached to me, Michael. You really don't need me anymore. And you are *never* alone."

Seine hugged me, projecting his final words. "Accept that you are bound by purpose. You have a purpose to fulfill before these Doors become your entrance to beyond the Beyond. Dedicate your Self to that, and with Treenie, your purpose will be your direction. Together, you will teach people how to reach their full potential of illumination, rather than continue to light candles in the dark." He smiled his love smile. "Besides, candles have a habit of flickering out." He turned away, then turned back to me. "People are asleep, Michael. Humanity is now making the transition from an age of illusion and separation into one of illumination and wholeness. To make this transition, you need to be awake." He smiled at me playfully. "I'm sure you can have fun waking people up. And as you know, this is not good-bye, Michael, just au revoir."

"I suppose if I were able to go with you, I would be parted from Treenie?"

"For a while, yes."

"Then it's okay. I would choose Treenie anyway."

Seine walked toward the Doors that I could not see. As he moved away from me, he became brighter, as though some inner sun was shining through him.

Despite what I said, I ran after him, caught by a sudden

impulse to pass through those Doors. However, as Seine suddenly became brilliantly illuminated and then swallowed up in the whitest, purest Light, my footsteps carried me with a rush back into my physical body.

*

My eyes fluttered, and a long, deep sigh escaped my lips as my awareness became centered in our everyday normality. Probably it was perfect timing, perhaps synchronism, but as I opened my eyes, Treenie walked into the room.

I looked at her, overwhelmed by all that had happened.

"Treenie . . . " My mind raced as a hundred thoughts and experiences crowded together, all wanting to be the first to be shared. My mouth opened, hesitated, then closed.

"I love you," I said.

Epilogue

A fter I finished writing this book, I went outside and walked for a while. I felt disturbed. This was not an easy book to write. I have learned that our view of life has become so very conditioned and limited that we see no more than a distortion of what Is. What I have shared in this book is a greater view, an enlargement on the brittle, crystalline structures of our everyday reality. My inner disturbance was only mild, but I pondered its cause.

It was drizzling, the light forest scrub dripping with overladen moisture. Mosquitoes buzzed into my face as I paced silently between a few trees, and I turned back. As I walked, my thoughts were on this book. I realized that the book contains an explosive potential. It is disruptive; it offers the reader a potential to burst from the restrictive bonds of illusion and self-deceit. And this can be painful. Did I have the right to inject pain and disruption into the lives of those who intuitively felt the truth of these pages?

A movement on the slim trunk of a sapling caught my eye. I watched as a cicada burst from its grotesque casing as an earthbound grub into a creature of the air, able to fly on powerful gossamer wings. I realized that this birthing was triggered by earlier heavy rains penetrating deep into the ground. For many years, the grub had been content with being a voracious creature of the soil, yet suddenly it was swept by the undeniable power of transformation.

I smiled in delight as I saw the connection, and my inner disturbance was stilled.

Before I reached my house, several thoughts had come to mind that I would like to share. All the books that I write are about Wholeness. Keeping this in mind, I would like you to read *Talking With Nature, Journey Into Nature,* and *Journey Into Oneness* as one book. It is a true account of my expansion of consciousness. And as it is for me, so it is for all humanity. Our way of expanding may well be different for each of us, but there are many common denominators. For example, we each create our own reality. Each of us has the power to create our own personal heaven or hell on earth. We have all been conditioned into living a lie. Very few people have learned that living a Truth is much easier than living a lie! Our suffering is a message from life that we are living a lie.

I could go on and on, but I would rather offer something that is constructive. I have learned that it is our focus in everyday living that determines the quality of our life. Our focus is registered in the main thrust of our thoughts and conversation. Let me offer you a simple but powerful exercise that you can use to transform your life. Remember, as with any exercise, you will receive from it in direct proportion to how much you put into it! So remove *all* judgment about yourself and others from your thoughts and your conversation. This will remove from your life all the blame you pile up on yourself and on other people—a very heavy burden. You will cease to be a victim in life, creating instead a far more positive reality. Also, focus on yourself as a divine Being of Light, perfect in every way possible. Think about your Lightness and talk about it. Stop referring to yourself as "me" or "I," and choose a description that uplifts and honors you. This will be challenging and changing. For example, refer to yourself as this Beautiful Being, this Radiant Person, or this Infinite Self. This is your Truth, and it will become your reality. As a metaphysical, multidimensional Being, you will be reprogramming your metaphysical universe/reality. We *all* have this inherent power of creation. Try it, and persist!

About the Author

Michael J. Roads was born in England, and from the time he was a child delving into the mysteries of a hidden, silent Nature, he has spent his life as an outdoorsman. His background is based in farming, and after marrying Treenie, they emigrated to Australia. During a decade of farming in Tasmania, Michael went through profound changes, gradually becoming attuned to the Spirit of the Land. This change was to take him away from farming and into a search for Self. Difficult years were to follow, but the inner search was unrelenting. To be free and to know Self was all that had meaning.

During this time, Michael and Treenie experienced community life, followed by a few years of Michael working as an organic farming consultant. Daily he focused on empowering his conscious spiritual connection with Nature. He learned to cross the membrane separating the material (physical) from the intangible (metaphysical). Writing about this experience became his creative outlet.

Michael's life now consists of writing and giving talks and seminars. He conducts three-hour mini-seminars, one-day seminars, and occasional one-week seminars throughout Australia, the United States, the United Kingdom, and Europe. He is a brilliant speaker. He is also "Awake." He speaks his truth clearly, without dogma or bias. He is funny, inspiring, and direct. He lives his truth. Above all, however, he is simple. He teaches no techniques, but, in his own words, "I teach people to practice reality until it overwhelms the illusions."

He has a dislike of organizations, and thus he belongs to none, nor will he allow any to form around him. He and Treenie are free spirits. They are, however, open to correspondence.

The Roadsway Tapes

These cassettes were recorded during some of Michael's talks, engendering all the impromptu interaction that a live audience invokes. They have not been edited, other than to ensure the vocal quality.

M1 The Spirit of Nature
M2 It's Time to Wake Up
M3 Taking Back Your Power
M4 Secret Principles for Living
M5 Higher Awareness of Organic Growing
T1 Treenie's Story (by Treenie)
M7–10 Becoming Free (a four-tape seminar)
M13 It's Time to Wake Up (a four-tape seminar)
M14 Becoming One With Nature
      (an eight-tape seminar)

About the Author

The cost of all single audio cassettes, including post and packing, is $U.S. 16.00 each. The cost of the four-tape seminar, "Becoming Free," is $U.S. 55.00. "It's Time to Wake Up" is also $U.S. 55.00. "Becoming One With Nature" is $U.S. 70.00.

Michael is also the author of *Talking With Nature, Journey Into Nature,* and *Simple Is Powerful* (all published in the U.S. by H J Kramer), and *The Natural Magic of Mulch,* published in Australia. *The Natural Magic of Mulch* is an acclaimed book on the philosophical and practical applications of organic, no-dig gardening. It covers cold, temperate, and subtropical climates. Its cost, including post and packing, is $U.S. 25.00.

For correspondence, public speaking and seminar information, the mulch book, or the tapes, please write to:

Michael and Treenie Roads
P.O. Box 778
Nambour, QLD, 4560
Australia

COMPATIBLE BOOKS

FROM H J KRAMER INC

TALKING WITH NATURE
by Michael J. Roads
"From Australia comes a major new writer . . . a magnificent
book!" —RICHARD BACH, Author, *Jonathan Livingston Seagull*

JOURNEY INTO NATURE
by Michael J. Roads
"If you only read one book this year, make that book
JOURNEY INTO NATURE." —FRIEND'S REVIEW

SIMPLE IS POWERFUL
by Michael J. Roads
Embarking on a search for meaning and freedom in their lives,
Michael and Treenie discover that answers are often deceptively simple.

WAY OF THE PEACEFUL WARRIOR
by Dan Millman
A tale of transformation and adventure . . . a worldwide best-seller.

SACRED JOURNEY OF THE PEACEFUL WARRIOR
by Dan Millman
"After you've read SACRED JOURNEY, you will know
what possibilities await you." —WHOLE LIFE TIMES

NO ORDINARY MOMENTS
by Dan Millman
Based on the premise that we can change our world by
changing ourselves, this book shares an approach to life that turns
obstacles into opportunities, and experiences into wisdom.

THE LIFE YOU WERE BORN TO LIVE:
A GUIDE TO FINDING YOUR LIFE PURPOSE
by Dan Millman
A modern method based on ancient wisdom that can help
you find new meaning, purpose, and direction in your life.

THE COMPLETE HOME GUIDE TO AROMATHERAPY
by Erich Keller
An easy-to-use guide to aromatherapy that opens
the door to the magical world of natural scents.

BRIDGE OF LIGHT
by LaUna Huffines
Tools of light for spiritual transformation—a spiritual classic.

THE BLUE DOLPHIN
by Robert Barnes
Based on current scientific understanding, THE BLUE DOLPHIN
is a poignant story of an exceptional dolphin,
and a powerful metaphor for human existence.

COMPATIBLE BOOKS

FROM H J KRAMER INC

THE EARTH LIFE SERIES
by Sanaya Roman
*A course in learning to live with joy,
sense energy, and grow spiritually.*

LIVING WITH JOY, BOOK I
*"I like this book because it describes the way I feel
about so many things."*—VIRGINIA SATIR

**PERSONAL POWER THROUGH AWARENESS:
A GUIDEBOOK FOR SENSITIVE PEOPLE, BOOK II**
"Every sentence contains a pearl. . . ."—LILIAS FOLAN

**SPIRITUAL GROWTH:
BEING YOUR HIGHER SELF, BOOK III**
*Orin teaches how to reach upward to align with the
higher energies of the universe, look inward to expand
awareness, and move outward in world service.*

An Orin/DaBen Book
CREATING MONEY
by Sanaya Roman and Duane Packer, Ph.D.
This best-selling book teaches advanced manifesting techniques.

**MESSENGERS OF LIGHT:
THE ANGELS' GUIDE TO SPIRITUAL GROWTH**
by Terry Lynn Taylor
*A light-hearted look at the angelic kingdom designed
to help you create heaven in your life.*

**GUARDIANS OF HOPE:
THE ANGELS' GUIDE TO PERSONAL GROWTH**
by Terry Lynn Taylor
GUARDIANS OF HOPE *brings the angels
down to earth with over sixty angel practices.*

**ANSWERS FROM THE ANGELS:
A BOOK OF ANGEL LETTERS**
by Terry Lynn Taylor
*Terry shares the letters she has received from people
all over the world that tell of their experiences with angels.*

CREATING WITH THE ANGELS
by Terry Lynn Taylor
*A journey into creativity including powerful
exercises and assistance from the angels.*